simply vegetarian

simply vegetarian

Sue Spitler

SIMPLY VEGETARIAN
is published by Surrey Books, Inc.
230 E. Ohio St., Suite 120, Chicago, IL 60611

First Edition 1 2 3 4 5

This book is manufactured in the United States of America

Library of Congress Cataloging-in-Publication Data

Spitler, Sue

    Simply Vegetarian / by Sue Spitler.—1st ed.
      p. cm.
    Includes index.
    ISBN 1-57284-023-4 (pbk.)
    1. Vegetarian cookery. 2. Low-calorie diet—Recipes. 3. Low-fat diet—Recipes.
    4. Low-cholesterol diet—Recipes. 5. Salt-free diet—Recipes. 1. Title.
    TX837.S714   1998
    641.5'636—dc21   98-27513
                         CIP

Illustrations © 1998 Patti Green
Editorial and production: Bookcrafters, Inc., Chicago
Design and typesetting: Joan Sommers Design, Chicago
Nutritional analyses: Linda R. Yoakam, M.S., R.D.

For free catalog and prices on quantity purchases, contact Surrey Books at the
address above

This title is distributed to the trade by Publishers Group West

Thank you, Pat Molden, for your help with yet another cookbook! I admire your culinary expertise, appreciate your wisdom, and most of all value your friendship. A big thanks to Susan Schwartz for making another cookbook possible, to Gene DeRoin for his proficient editing, and to Linda Yoakam, R.D., for providing nutritional analyses. A team effort to be applauded!

contents

introduction

Until a few years ago, vegetables were the last thing eaten on anybody's plate. That has changed today! Eating vegetarian is probably America's fastest growing food trend. It's a healthy way to eat and simply delicious!

Whether you're a "bona fide" vegetarian, an "occasional" vegetarian, or someone who just likes vegetables, this cookbook is perfect for you. *Simply Vegetarian* offers 130 recipes for anyone who enjoys cooking and desires excellent food but has little time to cook.

Recipes are coded so you can quickly tell whether they are vegan, lacto-ovo vegetarian, lacto-vegetarian, or ovo-vegetarian:

V (vegan)—recipes contain only plant-based food, with no dairy products or eggs.

LO (lacto-ovo vegetarian)—recipes contain dairy products and eggs.

L (lacto-vegetarian)—recipes contain dairy products, but no eggs.

O (ovo-vegetarian)—recipes contain eggs, but no dairy products.

PREPARATION AND COOKING TIMES

Knowing that busy lifestyles afford precious little cooking time, recipes in *Simply Vegetarian* are streamlined to get you in and out of the kitchen as quickly and effortlessly as possible. Recipes are easy to make, requiring no special skills or techniques. Ingredients are commonly available for easy 1-stop shopping. Many ingredients can be purchased packaged and ready-to-use; even produce can be purchased chopped, sliced, or shredded for ultimate convenience! Cooking methods are quick and easy, using a minimum of pots and pans.

Recipes in *Simply Vegetarian* can be prepared and ready to eat in 45 minutes or less, with preparation and cooking times given for each recipe. The 36 recipes in the Veg Express chapter can be prepared in just 20 minutes. Accomplishing this feat does require some agility on the part of the cook, however! It's necessary to be organized, and we're assuming that you'll take advantage of the purchased prepared foods we've indicated in recipes (also see Ingredients below). Read the recipe through and assemble equipment and ingredients before you start cooking—chef's hat optional!

Often part of the food preparation and the cooking are done simultaneously, for example, slicing eggplant for later use while onions and garlic are sauteing, or preparing ingredients for a pasta dish while the pasta is cooking. In such cases, the sauteing or pasta cooking time is considered part of the preparation time and is not calculated in total cooking time. In the Veg Express chapter, times are given as Prep/Cook Time, since preparation and cooking are mostly being done at the same time.

Two recipes in the Easy Entertaining chapter, Black Bean Cheesecake and Fettuccine Florentine Timbale, do require baking time which exceeds our 45-minute cooking limit. The baking time is untended, however, and allows time to relax with guests. These recipes were so delicious, they had to be included!

INGREDIENTS

Check your local grocery occasionally for new convenience food items. Literally hundreds of fresh, frozen, canned, and packaged new food products find their way to grocery shelves each year. An occasional visit to gourmet stores may garner specialty items to keep in your pantry or freezer for interesting menu additions.

Convenience foods used in *Simply Vegetarian* include:

Produce and Salad Bar Items

broccoli – florets, slaw
cabbage – slaw
carrots – peeled baby, sliced, shredded
cauliflower – florets
garlic – peeled whole cloves, chopped
   plain, roasted

mangoes – sliced
mushrooms – sliced
onions – chopped, sliced (fresh and
   frozen)
papayas – sliced

peppers, bell – chopped, stir-fry blend
(fresh and frozen)

pineapple – peeled

potatoes – quartered, shredded,
cubed, mashed, partially cooked
(refrigerated, frozen, dried)

salad greens – in a bag

spinach – in a bag

tomatoes – sun-dried (soft type that
don't require soaking)

vegetables – roasted, stir-fry (frozen)

Grocery Items

bread – crumbs, stuffing, croutons,
hot roll mix

cooking spray – vegetable, flavored
sprays, olive oil spray

fruit – canned and dried

grains – couscous, rice, millet, quinoa,
falafel mix, tabouleh mix, bulgur,
kasha

herb blends

lasagne noodles – no-boil

tomatoes – plain and seasoned

pasta – dried, refrigerated fresh

peppers – red bell roasted

pierogi – frozen and refrigerated

polenta – various flavors (refrigerated)

salad dressings – mixes and prepared

sauces – mixes and prepared

soup – vegetable broth

vegetables – canned

Dairy Items

cheeses and cheese blends –
reduced-fat, fat-free, shredded,
grated, crumbled, sliced

egg product – no-cholesterol

half-and-half – fat-free

milk – fat-free, 1% reduced-fat,
2% low-fat

NUTRITIONAL INFORMATION

Medical research increasingly supports the health benefits of including more fruits,
vegetables, grains, beans, breads, cereals, and pasta in our diets while limiting, if not
totally eliminating, meat, poultry, fish, dairy foods, and fats. Most recent recommenda-
tions from the U.S. Department of Agriculture suggest eating 6 to 11 servings of
bread, cereal, rice, or pasta per day; 2 to 4 servings of fruits; and 3 to 5 servings of
vegetables. Dr. Arlene Spark, professor of nutrition at the New York Medical College,
concurs with this information in her Vegetable Pyramid for vegetarian eating. In addition to the suggested servings in the 3 food groups above, the Vegetable Pyramid
includes 2 to 3 servings of milk products or milk substitutes, and 2 to 3 servings of
dry beans, nuts, seeds, peanut butter, soy products, or eggs daily. Special needs for

vegans, who eat only plant-based foods, include 2 tablespoons each of blackstrap molasses and brewer's yeast and 3 to 5 teaspoons of vegetable oil if extra calories are needed.

It's commonly thought that vegetarian cooking is high in fat due to ingredients such as nuts, cheese, or oil that are included as meat substitutes. Not true! Flavorful vegetarian cooking *can* be low in fat. Here, we've simply combined fresh foods and excellent quality fat-free, reduced-fat, reduced-sodium, and no-salt prepared products and used reduced-fat cooking methods to achieve delicious results.

The American Heart Association, National Academy of Sciences, National Cancer Institute, and American Diabetes Association all recommend that daily food intake consist of no more than 30% of calories from fat. The majority of our recipes meet or exceed that guideline. Our top limit per recipe is 35% calories from fat, with the consideration that a total day's meals will include other low-fat or non-fat foods to achieve a 30% average.

Specific nutritional information is provided for each recipe in this book, but nutritional data are not always infallible. The nutritional analyses are derived by using computer software highly regarded by nutritionists and dietitians, but they are meant to be used only as guidelines. Figures are based on actual laboratory values of ingredients, so results may vary slightly, depending upon the brand or manufacturer of an ingredient used.

Ingredients noted as "optional" or "to taste" or "for garnish" are not included in the nutritional analyses. When alternate choices or amounts of ingredients are given, the ingredient or amount listed first was used for analysis. Also, data are based on the first number of servings shown when a range is given. Nutritional analyses are also based on the reduced-fat cooking methods used; the addition of margarine, oil, or other ingredients to the recipes will invalidate data.

Other factors that can affect the accuracy of nutritional data include variability in sizes, weights, and measures of fruits, vegetables, and other foods. There is also a possible 20% error factor in the nutritional labeling of prepared foods. If you have any health problems that require strict dietary control, it is important to consult a physician, dietitian, or nutritionist before using recipes in this or any other cookbook. Also, if you are a diabetic or require a diet that restricts calories, fat, or sodium, remember that the nutritional data may be accurate for the recipe as written but not for the food you cooked due to the variables explained above.

everyday entrées

Asparagus Polenta Bake

Potatoes and Mushrooms au Gratin

Easy Eggplant Rotolo

3-Can Lasagne

Mexi-Can Lasagne

Root Veggies and Mashed Potatoes

Roasted Vegetables and Beans with Portobello Mushrooms

Roasted Vegetables with Mushroom Tortellini

Roasted Eggplant and Tomatoes with Ziti

Mediterranean Torta

Pierogi with Mushroom Sour Cream Sauce

Tempeh Fajitas

Orange-Scented Vegetables with Tempeh

Spring Vegetable Stir-Fry

Island Stew, Sweet-and-Sour

Chop Suey

Sweet Potato and Tempeh Patties

Personal Pizzas

Chipotle Potato and Egg Bake

Pancake Puff with Eggs Piperade

e v e r y d a y   e n t r é e s

ASPARAGUS POLENTA BAKE

A delicious dish that can be prepared a day in advance, then baked before serving; increase baking time 5 to 10 minutes.

6	ounces portobello mushrooms, thinly sliced
8	ounces asparagus, cut into 1-inch pieces
1–2	tablespoons olive oil
1	package (16 ounces) prepared Italian-herb polenta
1	cup water
1	ounce sun-dried tomatoes (not in oil), about 8 halves, sliced
½	cup (2 ounces) shredded Parmesan cheese

Saute mushrooms and asparagus in oil in large skillet 2 to 3 minutes; cook, covered, until asparagus is crisp-tender, about 5 minutes.

Mash polenta in medium saucepan; mix in water and cook over medium heat, whisking until smooth and hot, about 5 minutes. Stir in mushrooms and asparagus, and sun-dried tomatoes. Spoon mixture into 4 ramekins or a shallow casserole or quiche dish; sprinkle with Parmesan cheese.

Bake at 425 degrees until cheese is browned and polenta puffed, about 20 minutes.

TIP

If sun-dried tomatoes need to be softened, soak in hot water to cover for 5 to 10 minutes.

L

PREPARATION TIME:
15–20 minutes
BAKING TIME:
20 minutes
SERVINGS: *3–4*

PER SERVING:
Calories: 280
Protein (g): 14.3
Carbohydrate (g): 32.6
Fat (g): 10.9
Saturated Fat (g): 0.8
Cholesterol (mg): 12.6
Dietary Fiber (g): 4.5
Sodium (mg): 386

POTATOES AND MUSHROOMS AU GRATIN

L

PREPARATION TIME:
15–20 minutes

BAKING TIME:
20–30 minutes

SERVINGS: **6**

A time-savvy entrée that utilizes frozen and dried vegetables to speed preparation.

Vegetable cooking spray
½ red, *or* green, bell pepper, chopped
½ cup chopped onion
2 cups water
1½ cups frozen, *or* fresh, broccoli florets
½ cup frozen tiny peas
1½ ounces dried shiitake mushrooms, broken into
small pieces (about 6 mushrooms)
1 package (4½ ounces) dried julienned potatoes
¾ cup fat-free milk
1–1½ cups (4–6 ounces) shredded reduced-fat Swiss, *or* Cheddar, cheese

Spray medium saucepan with cooking spray; heat over medium heat until hot. Saute bell pepper and onion until tender, about 5 minutes. Add water, broccoli, peas, and dried mushrooms; heat to boiling.

Pour potato and sauce packet into 2-quart casserole; pour boiling vegetable mixture over and mix well. Stir in milk and cheese.

Bake, uncovered, at 400 degrees until golden, 20 to 30 minutes.

PER SERVING:
Calories: 191
Protein (g): 12.5
Carbohydrate (g): 28.7
Fat (g): 4.5
Saturated Fat (g): 2.1
Cholesterol (mg): 14.1
Dietary Fiber (g): 4.1
Sodium (mg): 572

EASY EGGPLANT ROTOLO

Incredibly simple to prepare, thanks to no-boil lasagne noodles!

L

8 no-boil lasagne noodles
Warm water
4 cups frozen stir-fry pepper blend
2 teaspoons minced garlic
1 tablespoon olive oil
1 small eggplant (about 1 pound), unpeeled, cut into $\frac{1}{2}$-inch cubes
1–2 teaspoons dried Italian seasoning
2 cups reduced-fat ricotta cheese
Salt and pepper, to taste
2 cans (14$\frac{1}{2}$ ounces each) diced tomatoes with crushed red pepper and basil
$\frac{1}{4}$ cup grated fat-free Parmesan cheese, *or* 1 cup (4 ounces) shredded
reduced-fat mozzarella cheese

PREPARATION TIME:
20–25 minutes
BAKING TIME:
20 minutes
SERVINGS: *4 (2 each)*

Arrange noodles in flat baking dish or pan and cover with warm water; let stand until noodles are softened, about 8 minutes. Drain well.

Saute pepper blend and garlic in oil in large skillet 3 to 4 minutes. Add eggplant and Italian seasoning and cook, covered, until eggplant is tender, about 10 minutes, stirring occasionally. Remove from heat and stir in ricotta cheese; season to taste with salt and pepper.

Spread $\frac{1}{2}$ cup vegetables and cheese mixture on each noodle and roll up. Arrange each rotolo, seam side down, in 13 x 9-inch baking pan. Pour tomatoes over and sprinkle with Parmesan cheese. Bake, uncovered, until hot through, about 20 minutes.

PER SERVING:
Calories: 398
Protein (g): 26.7
Carbohydrate (g): 55
Fat (g): 9.7
Saturated Fat (g): 4
Cholesterol (mg): 28.3
Dietary Fiber (g): 9.1
Sodium (mg): 1188

3-CAN LASAGNE

L

PREPARATION TIME:
10–15 minutes
BAKING TIME:
30 minutes
SERVINGS: *4 to 6*

The quickest, easiest lasagne ever because we use no-boil lasagne noodles and quality prepared food products.

> 6 no-boil lasagne noodles
> 1 can (15 ounces) cannellini, *or* Great Northern, beans, rinsed, drained, slightly mashed
> 1 cup reduced-fat cottage cheese
> 1 can (16 ounces) Italian-style zucchini with mushrooms and tomato sauce, undrained
> 1–1½ cups (4–6 ounces) shredded reduced-fat Italian 6-cheese blend, divided
> 1 can (14½ ounces) diced tomatoes with roasted garlic

Place 2 lasagne noodles in lightly greased 8-inch-square baking pan. Top with ½ the beans, ½ the cottage cheese, ½ the zucchini, and ⅓ cup shredded cheese. Repeat layers, ending with 2 lasagne noodles. Spoon diced tomatoes over top of lasagne.

Bake, covered with aluminum foil, at 375 degrees until noodles are fork-tender, about 30 minutes. Uncover and sprinkle with remaining ⅓ cup cheese; let stand 5 to 10 minutes before serving.

TIP

Any kind of beans can be substituted for the cannellini beans.

PER SERVING:
Calories: 361
Protein (g): 26
Carbohydrate (g): 51.5
Fat (g): 4.6
Saturated Fat (g): 2.4
Cholesterol (mg): 12.5
Dietary Fiber (g): 6.8
Sodium (mg): 1174

MEXI-CAN LASAGNE

This simple South-of-the-Border lasagne is one you'll say "ole" to!

L

   6 no-boil lasagne noodles
   1 can (15 ounces) vegetarian refried black beans
   1 can (11 ounces) nacho cheese soup
  1/3 cup fat-free milk
   1 tablespoon minced pickled jalapeño chili
  1/2 teaspoon ground cumin
   1 cup frozen, *or* canned, drained whole-kernel corn
   1 can (14 1/2 ounces) Mexican-seasoned stewed tomatoes
1/2 – 3/4 cup (2–3 ounces) shredded reduced-fat Monterey Jack, *or* Cheddar, cheese

Place 2 lasagne noodles in lightly greased 8-inch-square baking pan; top with 1/2 the refried beans. Mix cheese soup, milk, jalapeño chili, and cumin. Spoon 1/2 the cheese sauce over the beans and sprinkle with 1/2 the corn. Repeat layers, ending with 2 noodles. Spoon tomatoes over top of lasagne.

Bake, covered with aluminum foil, at 375 degrees until noodles are fork-tender, about 30 minutes. Uncover and sprinkle with shredded cheese; let stand 5 to 10 minutes before serving.

PREPARATION TIME:
10–15 minutes
BAKING TIME:
30 minutes
SERVINGS: *4 to 6*

PER SERVING:
Calories: 402
Protein (g): 20.9
Carbohydrate (g): 60.8
Fat (g): 10.4
Saturated Fat (g): 4.7
Cholesterol (mg): 20.3
Dietary Fiber (g): 8.8
Sodium (mg): 1319

ROOT VEGGIES AND MASHED POTATOES

L

PREPARATION TIME:
20 minutes

BAKING TIME:
25 minutes

SERVINGS: 4

(about 1½ cups each)

A selection of winter root vegetables, roasted to perfection and served with garlic-spiked mashed potatoes.

Vegetable cooking spray
3 medium beets, peeled, sliced
3 medium turnips, peeled, sliced
1 cup baby carrots
1 leek (white parts only), cut into 1-inch pieces
2½ cups halved Brussels sprouts
1 tablespoon caraway seeds
Salt and pepper, to taste
1½ pounds Idaho potatoes, unpeeled, cubed
4 cloves garlic, peeled
¼ cup 2% reduced-fat milk, hot
2 tablespoons margarine, cut in pieces

Line large jelly roll pan with aluminum foil; spray with cooking spray. Arrange beets, turnips, carrots, leek, and Brussels sprouts on pan in single layer; spray generously with cooking spray. Sprinkle vegetables with caraway seeds; sprinkle lightly with salt and pepper. Bake at 450 degrees until vegetables are tender and lightly browned, about 25 minutes.

While vegetables are roasting, cook potatoes and garlic in 2 inches simmering water in covered saucepan until tender, 10 to 15 minutes; drain. Mash potatoes and garlic with masher or electric mixer, adding milk and margarine. Season to taste with salt and pepper.

Spoon potatoes onto plates; spoon vegetables over potatoes.

PER SERVING:
Calories: 323
Protein (g): 10.4
Carbohydrate (g): 59.8
Fat (g): 6.9
Saturated Fat (g): 1.5
Cholesterol (mg): 1.1
Dietary Fiber (g): 10.9
Sodium (mg): 184

ROASTED VEGETABLES AND BEANS WITH PORTOBELLO MUSHROOMS

Roasting vegetables intensifies their natural flavor and sweetness; roasting time is cut in half with the new frozen roasted vegetable blends. Complement this full-flavored entrée with warm garlic bread.

PREPARATION TIME:

10–15 minutes

BAKING TIME:

30 minutes

SERVINGS: *4*

    Vegetable cooking spray

1 package (1 pound, 10 ounces) frozen Parmesan-herb oven-roasted vegetables

1 can (15 ounces) pinto beans, rinsed, drained

1 red, *or* green, bell pepper, cut into ½-inch strips

1 small onion, cut into thin wedges

2 tablespoons olive, *or* vegetable, oil, divided

4 large portobello mushrooms, stems removed (3 ounces each)

Line large jelly roll pan with aluminum foil; spray with cooking spray. Combine oven-roasted vegetables, beans, bell pepper, and onion on pan; drizzle with 1 tablespoon oil and toss.

Chop mushroom stems and add to vegetable mixture; sprinkle vegetables with seasoning packet. Brush mushroom caps with remaining 1 tablespoon oil and place at end of pan.

Bake at 450 degrees until browned, about 30 minutes, stirring mixed vegetables halfway through baking time. Arrange mushrooms on plates; spoon vegetables over.

PER SERVING:
Calories: 357
Protein (g): 8.9
Carbohydrate (g): 53.4
Fat (g): 9.4
Saturated Fat (g): 1.4
Cholesterol (mg): 5
Dietary Fiber (g): 11.2
Sodium (mg): 976

ROASTED VEGETABLES WITH MUSHROOM TORTELLINI

Substitute ravioli or a shaped pasta for the tortellini if you prefer.

PREPARATION TIME:
15 minutes

BAKING TIME:
30 minutes

SERVINGS: *4*

Vegetable cooking spray
3 medium Italian plum tomatoes
8 ounces small okra, ends trimmed
4 ounces small mushrooms
1 medium zucchini, cut into 1/4-inch slices
1 medium yellow summer squash, cut into 1/4-inch slices
4 ounces broccoli rabe, rinsed, dried, cut into 3-inch pieces, *or* broccoli florets
1 1/2 teaspoons dried Italian seasoning
Salt and pepper, to taste
1 package (9 ounces) fresh mushroom, *or* herb, tortellini, cooked, warm
1–2 tablespoons olive oil

Line large jelly roll pan with aluminum foil; spray with cooking spray. Cut each tomato into 6 wedges; cut wedges in half. Arrange tomatoes and remaining vegetables on jelly roll pan, keeping broccoli rabe at one end. Spray vegetables generously with cooking spray, and sprinkle with Italian seasoning and salt and pepper.

Roast vegetables at 450 degrees until tender and browned, about 30 minutes, removing broccoli rabe with spatula after about 20 minutes.

Combine vegetables and tortellini in serving bowl; drizzle with olive oil and toss.

PER SERVING:
Calories: 226
Protein (g): 10.5
Carbohydrate (g): 33.6
Fat (g): 7
Saturated Fat (g): 1.8
Cholesterol (mg): 10
Dietary Fiber (g): 6.4
Sodium (mg): 228

ROASTED EGGPLANT AND TOMATOES WITH ZITI

Canned diced tomatoes with roasted garlic replace winter's less-than-flavorful fresh tomatoes. Enjoy with any pasta, soft polenta, or in a warm pita.

V

PREPARATION TIME:
15 minutes
BAKING TIME:
25–30 minutes
SERVINGS: **4**

    Olive oil cooking spray
1 medium eggplant, unpeeled, cut into $\frac{1}{2}$-inch slices
3 medium onions, cut into $\frac{1}{2}$-inch wedges
$\frac{1}{2}$ teaspoon dried thyme leaves
$\frac{1}{2}$ teaspoon dried marjoram leaves
$\frac{1}{2}$ teaspoon dried savory leaves
    Salt and pepper, to taste
1 can ($14\frac{1}{2}$ ounces) diced tomatoes with roasted garlic
8 ounces ziti, cooked, warm

Line jelly roll pan with aluminum foil and spray with cooking spray. Cut eggplant slices into fourths; arrange on jelly roll pan with onions. Spray vegetables with cooking spray; sprinkle with herbs, salt, and pepper.

Roast vegetables at 450 degrees 20 minutes. Spoon tomatoes over vegetables, and roast until eggplant is tender, 5 to 10 minutes longer. Serve over ziti.

PER SERVING:
Calories: 298
Protein (g): 10.2
Carbohydrate (g): 62.4
Fat (g): 1.6
Saturated Fat (g): 0.2
Cholesterol (mg): 0
Dietary Fiber (g): 7.5
Sodium (mg): 414

MEDITERRANEAN TORTA

Hot roll mix makes this recipe no-fail and easy. Enjoy Mediterranean flavors in the colorful filling.

PREPARATION TIME:
15–20 minutes

BAKING TIME:
30 minutes

SERVINGS: *6*

PER SERVING:
Calories: 488
Protein (g): 17.7
Carbohydrate (g): 77.3
Fat (g): 11.6
Saturated Fat (g): 3.1
Cholesterol (mg): 43.7
Dietary Fiber (g): 5.2
Sodium (mg): 1319

1	package (16 ounces) hot roll mix
1	cup hot water
2	tablespoons margarine
1	egg
1	can (16 ounces) Italian-style zucchini with mushrooms and tomato sauce, undrained
1	can (15 ounces) garbanzo beans, rinsed, drained
1/3	cup raisins
1 1/2	teaspoons minced roasted garlic
1/2	teaspoon ground cinnamon
1/2	teaspoon ground cumin
1/2	teaspoon dried mint leaves
1/2–1	cup (2–4 ounces) shredded reduced-fat mozzarella cheese
2–4	ounces crumbled reduced-fat feta cheese

Make hot roll mix according to package directions, using hot water, margarine, and egg; let rise 10 to 15 minutes.

Combine remaining ingredients in bowl. Roll 3/4 of the dough on floured surface into 14-inch circle; ease dough into greased 8-inch springform pan, allowing edges to come to top of pan.

Spoon vegetable mixture into prepared pan. Fold edge of dough over vegetables. Roll remaining dough on floured surface to fit top of springform pan; place on top and crimp edges. Cut 1 or 2 slits in crust with sharp knife.

Bake at 400 degrees until dough is browned, about 25 to 30 minutes; cool on wire rack 5 to 10 minutes. Remove side of pan and cut into wedges.

PIEROGI WITH MUSHROOM SOUR CREAM SAUCE

The secret to the sauce is cooking the mushrooms very slowly until deeply browned, intensifying their flavor. Serve with any flavor fresh or frozen pierogi. Also delicious with ravioli or grilled eggplant slices!

L

PREP/COOK TIME:

25–30 minutes

SERVINGS: *4*

Vegetable cooking spray
12 ounces sliced mushrooms (about 6 cups)
¼ cup finely chopped onion
1 teaspoon minced garlic
¼ cup dry white wine, *or* vegetable broth
¼–½ teaspoon dried thyme leaves
¾ cup reduced-fat, *or* fat-free sour cream
Salt and pepper, to taste
2 packages (16 ounces each) fresh, *or* frozen, potato and onion pierogi
1 tablespoon margarine
1 tablespoon olive, *or* vegetable, oil
Minced parsley, for garnish

Spray large skillet with cooking spray; heat over medium heat until hot. Add mushrooms, onion, and garlic to skillet; spray generously with cooking spray and saute 1 to 2 minutes.

Add wine and thyme to skillet; heat to boiling. Reduce heat and simmer, covered, until mushrooms are very tender, about 5 minutes. Cook, uncovered, on medium-low heat until mushrooms are dry and well browned, about 15 minutes. Stir in sour cream; cook over medium-low heat 1 to 2 minutes. Season to taste with salt and pepper.

While mushrooms are cooking, cook pierogi in boiling water to cover in large saucepan until they float to the top, 3 to 5 minutes. Drain. Heat margarine and olive oil in large skillet; transfer pierogi to skillet and cook over medium heat until browned, 2 to 3 minutes on each side.

Arrange pierogi on serving plate; spoon Mushroom Sour Cream Sauce over and sprinkle with parsley.

PER SERVING:
Calories: 492
Protein (g): 16.3
Carbohydrate (g): 72.3
Fat (g): 14.1
Saturated Fat (g): 4.1
Cholesterol (mg): 43.4
Dietary Fiber (g): 5
Sodium (mg): 709

TEMPEH FAJITAS

L

PREPARATION TIME:
20 minutes
COOKING TIME:
15 minutes
SERVINGS: **6**
(2 fajitas each)

PER SERVING:
Calories: 427
Protein (g): 22.6
Carbohydrate (g): 62.5
Fat (g): 10.9
Saturated Fat (g): 1.6
Cholesterol (mg): 0
Dietary Fiber (g): 10.5
Sodium (mg): 903

Fajitas are an American interpretation of soft tacos. They can include any combination of vegetables you want.

8	ounces tempeh, cut into strips 2 x $\frac{1}{2}$ x $\frac{1}{2}$ inches
$\frac{1}{3}$	cup lime juice
1	tablespoon vegetable oil
1$\frac{1}{2}$	cups frozen stir-fry pepper blend
1	teaspoon minced garlic
1$\frac{1}{2}$	teaspoons ground cumin
1$\frac{1}{2}$	teaspoons dried oregano leaves
1	can (15 ounces) black beans, rinsed, drained
	Salt and pepper, to taste
12	flour, *or* corn, tortillas, warm
3	tablespoons finely chopped cilantro
1	cup mild, *or* medium, salsa
$\frac{3}{4}$	cup fat-free sour cream

Place tempeh in shallow glass baking dish; pour lime juice over. Let stand 20 minutes; drain.

Saute tempeh in oil in large skillet until browned, about 5 minutes; move tempeh to side of pan. Add pepper blend, garlic, and herbs; cook over medium heat until tender, about 5 minutes. Add beans; cook until hot, 2 to 3 minutes. Season to taste with salt and pepper.

Spoon mixture onto tortillas; sprinkle with cilantro, top with salsa and sour cream, and roll up.

ORANGE-SCENTED VEGETABLES
WITH TEMPEH

Both orange juice and rind are used to accent this dish. Substitute firm light tofu for the tempeh, if you like.

PREPARATION TIME:

15 minutes

COOKING TIME:

20 minutes

SERVINGS: *6*

 2 packages (8 ounces each) tempeh, cut into strips, *or* cubes
1½ cups orange juice
 2 teaspoons grated orange rind
 1 teaspoon minced garlic
 ¾ teaspoon dried marjoram leaves
 ½ teaspoon dried thyme leaves
 1 cinnamon stick (1-inch piece)
   Vegetable cooking spray
 1 large onion, sliced
 1 tablespoon flour
 3 medium tomatoes, chopped
 3 large carrots, cut into 1-inch pieces
 3 medium potatoes, unpeeled, cubed
   Salt and pepper, to taste

Arrange tempeh in shallow baking dish. Combine orange juice and rind, garlic, marjoram, thyme, and cinnamon stick and pour over tempeh. Let stand while preparing vegetables. Drain, reserving marinade.

Spray skillet with cooking spray; heat over medium heat until hot. Transfer tempeh to skillet and saute until browned, 2 to 3 minutes. Add onion and saute 5 minutes. Add flour and cook 1 to 2 minutes longer.

Add reserved marinade, tomatoes, carrots, and potatoes to skillet; heat to boiling. Reduce heat and simmer, covered, until vegetables are tender, about 10 minutes. Season to taste with salt and pepper.

PER SERVING:

Calories: 282
Protein (g): 19.1
Carbohydrate (g): 40.4
Fat (g): 6.5
Saturated Fat (g): 1.1
Cholesterol (mg): 0
Dietary Fiber (g): 9.7
Sodium (mg): 23

SPRING VEGETABLE STIR-FRY

This stir-fry is also great served over Chinese egg noodles, which cook in just 1 minute!

PREP/COOK TIME:

20–25 minutes

SERVINGS: **4**

1	package (6 1/4 ounces) fast-cooking long-grain and wild rice
1	cup frozen onion seasoning blend
1/2	package (20-ounce size) new potato wedges
1	cup sliced mushrooms
2	tablespoons vegetable oil
1	pound asparagus, cut into 1 1/2-inch pieces
1	teaspoon minced garlic
2–4	teaspoons minced gingerroot
1 1/2	cups vegetable broth
4	teaspoons cornstarch
1/4	cup cold water
1–2	teaspoons reduced-sodium tamari soy sauce
1	teaspoon sesame oil
	Salt and pepper, to taste
1	teaspoon toasted sesame seeds

PER SERVING:
Calories: 344
Protein (g): 11.8
Carbohydrate (g): 57.4
Fat (g): 9.6
Saturated Fat (g): 1.2
Cholesterol (mg): 0
Dietary Fiber (g): 5.9
Sodium (mg): 478

Cook rice according to package directions.

Stir-fry onion seasoning blend, potatoes, and mushrooms in oil in wok or large skillet over medium-high heat 3 to 5 minutes. Add asparagus, garlic, and gingerroot to wok; stir-fry 5 minutes.

Add broth to wok and heat to boiling; reduce heat and simmer, covered, until vegetables are crisp-tender, 3 to 5 minutes. Heat mixture to boiling; stir combined cornstarch and water into mixture. Boil, stirring constantly, until thickened, about 1 minute. Stir in soy sauce and sesame oil; season to taste with salt and pepper.

Spoon vegetable mixture over rice; sprinkle with sesame seeds.

ISLAND STEW, SWEET-AND-SOUR

Sweet-and-sour flavors team with tofu, pineapple, and beans for this island-inspired dish—delicious with jasmine rice or couscous.

2 packages (10½ ounces each) light tofu, cut into 1-inch cubes
1 tablespoon vegetable oil
3 cups frozen stir-fry pepper blend
2 teaspoons minced garlic
2 teaspoons minced gingerroot
1–2 jalapeño chilies, finely chopped
3 cups vegetable broth
1 can (20 ounces) pineapple chunks in juice, drained, juice reserved
2 tablespoons light brown sugar
2–3 teaspoons curry powder
2–3 tablespoons apple cider vinegar
2 tablespoons cornstarch
1 can (15 ounces) black beans, rinsed, drained

Cook tofu in oil in large skillet over medium heat until browned on all sides, about 8 minutes. Remove from skillet.

Add pepper blend, garlic, gingerroot, and jalapeño chilies to skillet; saute 5 minutes. Stir in broth, pineapple (reserve juice), sugar, curry powder, vinegar, and tofu; heat to boiling. Reduce heat and simmer, uncovered, 5 minutes.

Heat mixture to boiling. Mix cornstarch and reserved pineapple juice; stir into boiling mixture. Boil, stirring frequently, until mixture is thickened, about 1 minute. Stir in beans; cook over medium heat 2 to 3 minutes longer.

PREP/COOK TIME:
30–35 minutes
SERVINGS: **6**
(about 1¼ cups each)

PER SERVING:
Calories: 228
Protein (g): 11.8
Carbohydrate (g): 37.4
Fat (g): 4.7
Saturated Fat (g): 0.3
Cholesterol (mg): 0
Dietary Fiber (g): 6.6
Sodium (mg): 812

CHOP SUEY

V

PREP/COOK TIME:

25–30 minutes

SERVINGS: **6**

Bead molasses, a very dark molasses, adds the traditional flavor accent to this dish. Dark molasses can be substituted.

1½ packages (8 ounces each) tempeh, cut into strips, *or* cubes

2–3 tablespoons tamari soy sauce

1–2 teaspoons peanut, *or* vegetable, oil

2 cups frozen stir-fry pepper blend

1 teaspoon minced garlic

2 cups thinly sliced Chinese cabbage, *or* 1 cup sliced celery

1 cup sliced mushrooms

1½ cups vegetable broth

2 tablespoons cornstarch

½–1 tablespoon bead molasses, *or* dark unsulfured molasses

2 cups fresh, *or* canned, rinsed, drained bean sprouts

½–1 can (8 ounces) rinsed, drained bamboo shoots

½–1 can (8 ounces) rinsed, drained water chestnuts

Pepper, to taste

4 cups cooked white rice, warm

PER SERVING:
Calories: 317
Protein (g): 18.5
Carbohydrate (g): 49.4
Fat (g): 6
Saturated Fat (g): 1
Cholesterol (mg): 0
Dietary Fiber (g): 7.3
Sodium (mg): 602

Brush tempeh with soy sauce; let stand while preparing other ingredients.

Stir-fry tempeh in oil in wok or large skillet until browned, 3 to 4 minutes; remove.

Add pepper blend and garlic to wok; saute 2 to 3 minutes. Add cabbage and mushrooms; stir-fry until vegetables are crisp-tender, 3 to 5 minutes longer.

Mix broth, cornstarch, and molasses; stir into wok and heat to boiling. Boil, stirring constantly, until thickened, 1 to 2 minutes. Stir in tempeh, bean sprouts, bamboo shoots, and water chestnuts; cook until hot through, about 2 minutes. Season to taste with pepper. Serve with rice.

SWEET POTATO AND TEMPEH PATTIES

Use cornbread stuffing crumbs in this recipe if you can, as they add great flavor and texture to the patties.

L

PREPARATION TIME:
15–20 minutes
COOKING TIME:
10 minutes
SERVINGS: **4**

- ½ cup chopped onion
- ½ cup chopped red bell pepper
- ½ jalapeño chili, minced
- 2 teaspoons minced garlic
- 1–2 teaspoons vegetable oil
- 1 package (8 ounces) tempeh, crumbled
- 1 can (15 ounces) sweet potatoes, drained, mashed (1½ cups)
- 2 tablespoons apricot spreadable fruit
- 1 cup cornbread stuffing crumbs
  Salt and pepper, to taste
- ½ cup applesauce
- ½ cup reduced-fat sour cream

Saute onion, bell pepper, jalapeño chili, and garlic in oil in large skillet 2 to 3 minutes. Add tempeh to skillet; cook until vegetables are tender, 5 to 8 minutes. Remove from heat; stir in sweet potatoes and spreadable fruit.

Crush stuffing crumbs with rolling pin to make fine crumbs; stir ⅔ cup crumbs into vegetable mixture, reserving remaining crumbs. Season to taste with salt and pepper. Shape mixture into patties; coat with reserved crumbs.

Cook patties over medium heat in greased large skillet until browned, about 5 minutes on each side. Serve patties warm with applesauce and sour cream.

PER SERVING:
Calories: 338
Protein (g): 16.9
Carbohydrate (g): 50.5
Fat (g): 8.7
Saturated Fat (g): 3
Cholesterol (mg): 10
Dietary Fiber (g): 8.4
Sodium (mg): 172

PERSONAL PIZZAS

L

A pizza apiece, perfect with a salad for lunch, brunch, or a hearty snack. Toppings can vary according to what your refrigerator offers—be creative and have fun!

PREPARATION TIME:
15 minutes

BAKING TIME:
18–20 minutes

SERVINGS: *8*

1 package (1 pound, 13 ounces) large reduced-fat buttermilk biscuits
1 can (15 ounces) red kidney beans, rinsed, drained
½ cup chopped roasted red bell pepper
4 canned, drained artichoke hearts, coarsely chopped
4 ounces asiago, *or* Parmesan, cheese, shredded
2 teaspoons dried Italian seasoning, divided
4 Italian plum tomatoes, thinly sliced
Salt and pepper, to taste

Roll biscuits into 6-inch rounds and place on greased baking sheet. Combine beans, roasted red bell pepper, artichoke hearts, cheese, and 1 teaspoon Italian seasoning in bowl; spoon onto biscuits.

Top each pizza with tomato slices; sprinkle lightly with salt, pepper, and remaining 1 teaspoon Italian seasoning. Bake at 350 degrees until biscuits are browned, 18 to 20 minutes.

PER SERVING:
Calories: 452
Protein (g): 16.3
Carbohydrate (g): 58.5
Fat (g): 16.4
Saturated Fat (g): 6.1
Cholesterol (mg): 11.2
Dietary Fiber (g): 4.8
Sodium (mg): 1555

CHIPOTLE POTATO AND EGG BAKE

Perfect for brunch, this recipe boasts the convenience of frozen vegetable products. One-half cup each sliced red, yellow, and green bell peppers and onion can be substituted for the frozen stir-fry pepper blend.

L

	Vegetable cooking spray
2	cups frozen stir-fry pepper blend
1–2	teaspoons minced garlic
½–1	small canned chipotle chili in adobo sauce, chopped
1⅓	cups fat-free milk
2⅔	cups frozen mashed potatoes
	Salt, to taste
4	eggs
½–¾	cup (2–3 ounces) shredded reduced-fat Cheddar cheese

Spray medium saucepan with cooking spray; heat over medium heat until hot. Saute pepper blend and garlic until liquid is evaporated and peppers begin to brown, about 5 minutes. Add chipotle chili and milk; heat until milk is steaming. Stir potatoes into mixture; cook over medium heat, stirring frequently, until potatoes are thickened, 4 to 5 minutes. Season to taste with salt.

Spread potato mixture in 8-inch-square, or round, baking pan, or use 4 individual gratin dishes. Make 4 indentations in potatoes with back of spoon; break eggs into indentations. Sprinkle cheese over potatoes and eggs.

Bake at 350 degrees until eggs are desired doneness, 13 to 15 minutes.

TIP

For a serving variation, potato mixture can be spooned onto serving plates and topped with poached or fried eggs.

PREPARATION TIME:
15–20 minutes
BAKING TIME:
13–15 minutes
SERVINGS: **4**

PER SERVING:
Calories: 284
Protein (g): 19.2
Carbohydrate (g): 36
Fat (g): 8.3
Saturated Fat (g): 3.6
Cholesterol (mg): 221.5
Dietary Fiber (g): 3.9
Sodium (mg): 649

PANCAKE PUFF WITH EGGS PIPERADE

PREPARATION TIME:
15–20 minutes

BAKING TIME:
20 minutes

SERVINGS: **4**

PER SERVING:
Calories: 344
Protein (g): 23.5
Carbohydrate (g): 30.3
Fat (g): 13.6
Saturated Fat (g): 3.6
Cholesterol (mg): 319
Dietary Fiber (g): 2
Sodium (mg): 495

A puffed Dutch Pancake is a wonderful serving bowl for chili-inspired scrambled eggs.

Dutch Pancake (see pg. 149)
Vegetable cooking spray
2 cups frozen stir-fry pepper blend
½–1 jalapeño chili, minced
1 teaspoon minced garlic
1 small tomato, chopped
4 eggs
1 cup no-cholesterol egg product, *or* 8 egg whites
2 tablespoons fat-free milk
Salt and pepper, to taste
Minced parsley, *or* chives, for garnish

Make Dutch Pancake.

Spray skillet with cooking spray; heat over medium heat until hot. Saute stir-fry pepper blend, jalapeño chili, and garlic until tender, 5 to 8 minutes; stir in tomato.

Whisk eggs, egg product, and milk until well blended. Add eggs to skillet and cook over medium heat until set, stirring frequently. Add salt and pepper to taste. Spoon into hot Dutch Pancake and garnish with parsley.

veg
express

Hearty Corn and Potato Chowder

Bean-Thickened Soup

Garden Harvest Soup

Bean Gazpacho

Three-Bean Stew with Polenta

Spiced Bean Stew with Fusilli

Garden Vegetable and Tempeh Saute

Garden Stew with Couscous

Very Quick Bean and Vegetable Stew

Vegetables Paprikash

Stewed Black-Eyed Peas and Beans

Fettuccine with Fresh Fennel and Sprouts

Creamy Vegetable and "Beef" Stroganoff

Wine-Glazed Ravioli and Asparagus

Light Summer Pasta

20-Minute Ravioli

Pasta and Portobello Mushrooms Vinaigrette

Mafalde with Garbanzo Beans, Fresh Tomatoes, and Croutons

Black Bean and Smoked Tofu Salad

Creamy Fettuccine Primavera

Great Garlic Pasta

Asparagus and White Beans, Italian-Style

Italian-Style Beans and Vegetables

Eggplant and Vegetable Saute

Vegetable Curry

Thai Fried Rice

Thai Stir-Fry

Sesame Asparagus Stir-Fry

Meatless Sloppy Joes

Cranberry Cheese Melt

Falafel "Burgers"

Mesquite Hash and Eggs

Sweet Potato Hash and Eggs

Breakfast Burritos

Very Berry Smoothie

Tofruity

veg express

HEARTY CORN AND POTATO CHOWDER

If you don't mind a few minutes extra preparation time, cut corn fresh from the cob for this delicious soup.

PREP/COOK TIME:
20 minutes
SERVINGS: **4**
(about 2 cups each)

  2 cups frozen, *or* canned, drained whole-kernel corn
  ¾ cup chopped onion
  1 tablespoon vegetable oil
  2 cups vegetable broth
  3 cups cubed, unpeeled Idaho potatoes
  ½ cup sliced celery
  ½ teaspoon dried thyme leaves
1¾ cups 2% reduced-fat milk
    Salt and pepper, to taste
    Finely chopped parsley and chives, for garnish

Saute corn and onion in oil in large saucepan 2 to 3 minutes. Process ½ the vegetable mixture and the broth in food processor or blender until finely chopped. Return mixture to saucepan.

Add potatoes, celery, and thyme leaves to saucepan; heat to boiling. Reduce heat and simmer, covered, until vegetables are tender, about 10 minutes. Stir in milk; cook until hot through, 2 to 3 minutes. Season to taste with salt and pepper. Pour soup into bowls; sprinkle with parsley and chives.

TIP

If thicker soup is desired, mix 2 to 3 tablespoons flour with ⅓ cup water. Heat soup to boiling; stir in flour mixture and boil, stirring constantly, until thickened, about 1 minute.

PER SERVING:
Calories: 339
Protein (g): 10.8
Carbohydrate (g): 64.2
Fat (g): 6.6
Saturated Fat (g): 1.8
Cholesterol (mg): 8
Dietary Fiber (g): 5.3
Sodium (mg): 579

BEAN-THICKENED SOUP

A very quick and easy soup that's almost fat free! The pureed beans contribute a hearty texture and subtle flavor.

1	large Idaho potato, unpeeled, cut into $\frac{1}{2}$-inch cubes
2	carrots, sliced
$\frac{1}{2}$	cup chopped onion
$1\frac{1}{2}$	teaspoons minced garlic
2	tablespoons vegetable oil
2	cans (15 ounces each) Great Northern beans, rinsed, drained, divided
$1\frac{3}{4}$	cups vegetable broth, divided
1	can (16 ounces) diced tomatoes, undrained
$\frac{1}{4}-\frac{1}{2}$	teaspoon dried thyme leaves
$\frac{1}{2}-\frac{3}{4}$	teaspoon dried sage leaves
	Salt and pepper, to taste

Saute potatoes, carrots, onion, and garlic in oil in large saucepan for 5 minutes.

Process 1 can beans and half the broth in a food processor or blender until smooth. Add to sauteed vegetables along with remaining broth, beans, tomatoes, and herbs. Heat to boiling; reduce heat and simmer, covered, until vegetables are tender, about 10 minutes. Season to taste with salt and pepper.

V

PREP/COOK TIME:
20 minutes
SERVINGS: *4*
(about 1 $\frac{1}{2}$ cups each)

PER SERVING:
Calories: 262
Protein (g): 13.4
Carbohydrate (g): 46.8
Fat (g): 7.5
Saturated Fat (g): 0.9
Cholesterol (mg): 0
Dietary Fiber (g): 12.7
Sodium (mg): 1555

GARDEN HARVEST SOUP

L

PREP/COOK TIME:
20 minutes
SERVINGS: *4*
(about 2 cups each)

Vary the vegetables according to your garden harvest or greengrocer's bounty.

¾ cup chopped onion
1 teaspoon minced garlic
1 tablespoon olive oil
5 cups vegetable broth
1½ cups baby carrots
¼ package (22-ounce size) new potato wedges
2 cups fresh, *or* canned, drained whole-kernel corn
½ cup whole milk
1 cup halved green beans
2 medium zucchini, sliced
1 teaspoon dried Italian seasoning
Salt and pepper, to taste

Saute onion and garlic in oil in large saucepan over medium heat 2 to 3 minutes. Add remaining ingredients, except salt and pepper; heat to boiling. Reduce heat and simmer, covered, until vegetables are tender, about 10 minutes. Season to taste with salt and pepper.

PER SERVING:
Calories: 220
Protein (g): 8.4
Carbohydrate (g): 38.9
Fat (g): 6.2
Saturated Fat (g): 1.2
Cholesterol (mg): 4.2
Dietary Fiber (g): 5.9
Sodium (mg): 1315

BEAN GAZPACHO

Pureed beans contribute a creamy texture and subtle flavor to this nutrition-packed gazpacho.

V

PREPARATION TIME:
10–15 minutes
SERVINGS: *8*
(about 1 1/3 cups each)

3	cans (15 ounces each) pinto beans, rinsed, drained, divided
3–4	cups tomato juice
3–4	tablespoons lime juice
2	teaspoons Worcestershire sauce
8	ice cubes
1	jar (16 ounces) thick and chunky mild, *or* medium, salsa
1	cup chopped cucumber
1	cup thinly sliced celery
1/2	cup chopped onion
1/2	cup chopped green bell pepper
2	teaspoons minced roasted garlic
	Salt and pepper, to taste
1/2	small avocado, peeled, pitted, chopped
1 1/2	cups unseasoned croutons

Process 1/2 the beans, 3 cups tomato juice, lime juice, Worcestershire sauce, and ice cubes in food processor or blender until smooth; pour into large bowl. Mix in remaining ingredients, except avocado and croutons; add additional tomato juice if desired for consistency. Season to taste with salt and pepper.

Mix avocado into soup and pour into bowls; sprinkle with croutons.

PER SERVING:
Calories: 215
Protein (g): 21.9
Carbohydrate (g): 37.1
Fat (g): 3.8
Saturated Fat (g): 0.4
Cholesterol (mg): 0.1
Dietary Fiber (g): 13.4
Sodium (mg): 2567

THREE-BEAN STEW WITH POLENTA

V

PREP/COOK TIME:

20 minutes

SERVINGS: 4

(about 1 cup each)

Use any kind of canned or cooked dried beans that you like; one 15-ounce can of drained beans yields 1½ cups of beans. Many flavors of prepared polenta are now available in the produce department.

1	cup chopped onion
½	cup chopped red, *or* green, bell pepper
1–2	tablespoons olive oil
1	tablespoon flour
1	can (15 ounces) black-eyed peas, rinsed, drained
1	can (15 ounces) black beans, rinsed, drained
1	can (15 ounces) red beans, rinsed, drained
1	can (14½ ounces) diced tomatoes with roasted garlic, undrained
¾	teaspoon dried sage leaves
½	teaspoon dried rosemary leaves
2–3	cups vegetable broth, divided
	Salt and pepper, to taste
1½	packages (16-ounce size) prepared polenta

Saute onion and bell pepper in oil in large saucepan 2 to 3 minutes. Stir in flour; cook 1 minute longer.

Add beans, tomatoes and liquid, herbs, and 1 cup of broth to saucepan; heat to boiling. Reduce heat and simmer, covered, 10 minutes. Season to taste with salt and pepper.

While stew is simmering, mix polenta in medium saucepan with enough additional broth to achieve desired consistency. Heat over medium heat until hot. Spoon polenta into shallow bowls; spoon stew over.

PER SERVING:

Calories: 498

Protein (g): 24.7

Carbohydrate (g): 86.9

Fat (g): 8.6

Saturated Fat (g): 1.6

Cholesterol (mg): 3.4

Dietary Fiber (g): 20.3

Sodium (mg): 2558

SPICED BEAN STEW WITH FUSILLI

Use any favorite beans or pasta shapes in this versatile chili.

8 ounces fusilli
2 cups chopped onions
½ cup sliced celery
1 cup sliced mushrooms
1–2 tablespoons vegetable oil
2 cans (14½ ounces each) diced tomatoes with roasted garlic
1 can (15½ ounces) garbanzo beans, rinsed, drained
1 can (15 ounces) dark red kidney beans, rinsed, drained
1–2 tablespoons chili powder
1–2 teaspoons ground cumin
¾ teaspoon dried oregano leaves
Salt and pepper, to taste
3–4 tablespoons sliced green, *or* ripe, olives

Cook fusilli according to package directions. While it is cooking . . .

Saute onions, celery, and mushrooms in oil in large saucepan 5 minutes. Add tomatoes, beans, and herbs. Heat to boiling. Reduce heat and simmer, covered, until vegetables are tender, about 10 minutes. Stir in pasta. Season to taste with salt and pepper. Serve stew in bowls; sprinkle with olives.

V

PREP/COOK TIME:

20 minutes

SERVINGS: *8*

(about 1¼ cups each)

PER SERVING:
Calories: 265
Protein (g): 10.6
Carbohydrate (g): 47.5
Fat (g): 4.1
Saturated Fat (g): 0.6
Cholesterol (mg): 0
Dietary Fiber (g): 8.9
Sodium (mg): 1004

GARDEN VEGETABLE AND TEMPEH SAUTE

Vary the vegetables according to season and availability. Serve over rice, fresh Chinese-style noodles, or pasta, if desired.

PREP/COOK TIME:
20 minutes
SERVINGS: **4**
(about 1 1/4 cups each)

2 cups frozen stir-fry pepper blend
1 teaspoon minced garlic
1 tablespoon olive oil
1 package (8 ounces) tempeh, cut into 1/2-inch cubes
1 cup tomato juice
2 tablespoons tamari soy sauce
1 medium zucchini, sliced
2 cups (4 ounces) sliced mushrooms
1 teaspoon dried basil leaves
1 teaspoon dried oregano leaves
1/4 teaspoon cayenne pepper
2 medium tomatoes, cut into wedges
   Salt, to taste

PER SERVING:
Calories: 199
Protein (g): 15.6
Carbohydrate (g): 19.2
Fat (g): 8.4
Saturated Fat (g): 1.3
Cholesterol (mg): 0
Dietary Fiber (g): 7.8
Sodium (mg): 732

Saute pepper blend and garlic in oil in large skillet 2 to 3 minutes. Add tempeh and cook 5 minutes. Stir in remaining ingredients, except tomatoes and salt; heat to boiling. Reduce heat and simmer, covered, until vegetables are tender, about 5 minutes.

Add tomato wedges; cook, covered, until softened, about 2 to 3 minutes. Season to taste with salt.

GARDEN STEW WITH COUSCOUS

Take advantage of your garden's bounty with this quick and easy stew, substituting vegetables you have in abundance.

Garlic-flavor vegetable cooking spray
2 medium onions, cut into 1-inch pieces
8 ounces shiitake, *or* white mushrooms, sliced
1 small jalapeño chili, finely chopped
1 tablespoon flour
2 cups vegetable broth
2 medium zucchini, sliced
1 medium turnip, cut into ¼-inch cubes
8 ounces baby carrots
2 packages (5.9 ounces each) couscous
4 medium tomatoes, coarsely chopped
½ cup loosely packed cilantro leaves
Salt and pepper, to taste

Spray large saucepan with cooking spray; heat over medium heat until hot. Saute onions, mushrooms, and jalapeño chili 2 to 3 minutes. Stir in flour; cook 1 minute longer.

Add broth, zucchini, turnip, and carrots to saucepan; heat to boiling. Reduce heat and simmer, covered, until vegetables are tender, 10 to 12 minutes.

While stew is simmering, cook couscous according to package directions, discarding spice packet.

Add tomatoes and cilantro to stew; season to taste with salt and pepper. Serve with couscous.

V

PREP/COOK TIME:
20 minutes
SERVINGS: *6*
(about 1½ cups each)

PER SERVING:
Calories: 301
Protein (g): 10.8
Carbohydrate (g): 63.5
Fat (g): 1.4
Saturated Fat (g): 0.2
Cholesterol (mg): 0
Dietary Fiber (g): 7
Sodium (mg): 378

VERY QUICK BEAN AND VEGETABLE STEW

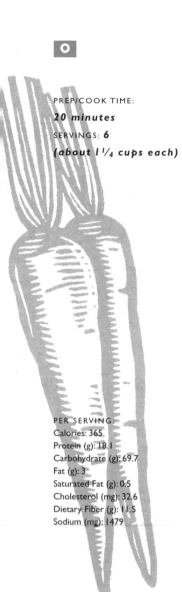

Pureed beans provide a perfect thickening for the stew, and canned vegetables make it extra quick.

PREP/COOK TIME:
20 minutes
SERVINGS: **6**
(about 1¼ cups each)

8	ounces egg noodles
	Vegetable cooking spray
3	carrots, sliced
¾	cup chopped onion
2	teaspoons minced garlic
1	can (15 ounces) navy beans, rinsed, drained
2	cups vegetable broth, divided
2	cans (16 ounces each) Italian-style zucchini with mushrooms in tomato sauce
1	can (15 ounces) black beans, rinsed, drained
1	cup frozen peas
1½	teaspoons dried Italian seasoning
	Salt and pepper, to taste

Cook noodles according to package directions. While they are cooking ...

Spray large saucepan with cooking spray; heat over medium heat until hot. Saute carrots, onion, and garlic 5 minutes. Puree navy beans with half the broth in blender. Add to sauteed vegetables in saucepan. Add remaining broth, zucchini, black beans, peas, and Italian seasoning.

Heat to boiling. Reduce heat and simmer, uncovered, until vegetables are tender, about 10 minutes. Season to taste with salt and pepper. Spoon stew over noodles in shallow bowls.

PER SERVING:
Calories: 365
Protein (g): 18.1
Carbohydrate (g): 69.7
Fat (g): 3
Saturated Fat (g): 0.5
Cholesterol (mg): 32.6
Dietary Fiber (g): 11.5
Sodium (mg): 1479

VEGETABLES PAPRIKASH

Your preference of hot or sweet paprika can be used in this recipe. Serve over any flat pasta or rice.

12 ounces egg noodles
   Vegetable cooking spray
4 cups packaged coleslaw mix
1 cup chopped onion
1 medium zucchini, sliced
1½ cups sliced mushrooms
1 medium tomato, chopped
3 tablespoons flour
1 tablespoon paprika
¾ cup vegetable broth
½ cup reduced-fat sour cream
   Salt and pepper, to taste

PREP/COOK TIME:

20 minutes

SERVINGS: 4

Cook noodles according to package directions. While they are cooking . . .

Spray large skillet with cooking spray and heat over medium heat until hot. Cook coleslaw, onion, and zucchini, covered, 5 to 8 minutes. Add mushrooms and tomato. Cook over medium heat, covered, until mushrooms and tomato are wilted, about 2 minutes.

Stir in flour and paprika; cook 1 to 2 minutes, stirring constantly. Stir in broth; heat to boiling. Boil, stirring constantly, until sauce thickens, about 1 minute. Stir in sour cream; season to taste with salt and pepper. Serve over noodles.

PER SERVING:
Calories: 416
Protein (g): 16.5
Carbohydrate (g): 74
Fat (g): 6.7
Saturated Fat (g): 2.8
Cholesterol (mg): 83.4
Dietary Fiber (g): 6.3
Sodium (mg): 242

STEWED BLACK-EYED PEAS AND BEANS

PREP/COOK TIME:
20 minutes
SERVINGS: **6**
(about 1¼ cups each)

PER SERVING:
Calories: 235
Protein (g): 12.1
Carbohydrate (g): 43.1
Fat (g): 3.6
Saturated Fat (g): 0.5
Cholesterol (mg): 0
Dietary Fiber (g): 10.1
Sodium (mg): 973

A hearty stew that can be made in 20 minutes with pantry staples. Serve with warm biscuits or cornbread.

1½	cups chopped onions
1	teaspoon minced garlic
1	tablespoon olive oil
1	can (28 ounces) diced tomatoes, undrained
1	can (19 ounces) garbanzo beans, rinsed, drained
1	can (15½ ounces) black-eyed peas, rinsed, drained
1	package (10 ounces) frozen spinach
2	cups frozen cut okra
1	teaspoon dried marjoram leaves
¾	teaspoon dried thyme leaves
¼	teaspoon hot pepper sauce
	Salt and pepper, to taste

Saute onions and garlic in oil in large saucepan 2 to 3 minutes. Stir in remaining ingredients, except salt and pepper; heat to boiling. Reduce heat and simmer, covered, until okra is tender, about 10 minutes. Season to taste with salt and pepper.

FETTUCCINE WITH FRESH FENNEL AND SPROUTS

Brussels sprouts cook more quickly when halved.

L

PREP/COOK TIME:

15–20 minutes

SERVINGS: *4*

8 ounces spinach fettuccine

Olive oil cooking spray

1 fennel bulb, thinly sliced

1 medium onion, thinly sliced

8 ounces small Brussels sprouts, halved

¼ cup water, *or* vegetable broth

1 tablespoon lemon juice

Salt and pepper, to taste

2 ounces Parmesan cheese, shredded, *or* shaved

4 tablespoons toasted pine nuts, *or* slivered almonds

Cook fettuccine according to package directions. While pasta is cooking . . .

Spray large skillet with cooking spray; heat over medium heat until hot. Saute fennel and onion 3 to 4 minutes. Add Brussels sprouts and water and heat to boiling; reduce heat and simmer, covered, until sprouts are crisp-tender, 5 to 8 minutes. Stir in lemon juice; season to taste with salt and pepper.

Spoon fennel and sprouts mixture over pasta on serving platter; sprinkle with Parmesan cheese and pine nuts.

PER SERVING:
Calories: 337
Protein (g): 18.2
Carbohydrate (g): 41.1
Fat (g): 12.3
Saturated Fat (g): 4.2
Cholesterol (mg): 78.1
Dietary Fiber (g): 5.8
Sodium (mg): 360

CREAMY VEGETABLE AND "BEEF" STROGANOFF

PREP/COOK TIME:
20 minutes
SERVINGS: *8*
(about 1 cup each)

PER SERVING:
Calories: 363
Protein (g): 20.2
Carbohydrate (g): 53.2
Fat (g): 7.4
Saturated Fat (g): 3.1
Cholesterol (mg): 61.3
Dietary Fiber (g): 6.1
Sodium (mg): 207

Purchased sliced mushrooms and broccoli florets speed preparation time for this stew. For a rich flavor variation, use wild mushrooms.

16	ounces egg noodles
2	medium onions, thinly sliced
12	ounces sliced mushrooms
1	teaspoon minced garlic
1	tablespoon vegetable oil
$\frac{1}{4}$	cup dry red wine, *or* water
12	ounces broccoli florets and sliced stalks
$\frac{3}{4}$	package (12-ounce size) frozen pre-browned vegetable protein crumbles
1	cup 2% reduced-fat milk
2	tablespoons flour
$1\frac{1}{2}$	teaspoons Dijon-style mustard
1	cup reduced-fat sour cream
$\frac{1}{2}$	teaspoon dried dill weed
	Salt and white pepper, to taste

Cook noodles according to package directions. While they are cooking . . .

Saute onions, mushrooms, and garlic in oil in large skillet until softened, about 5 minutes. Add wine, broccoli, and protein crumbles; heat to boiling. Reduce heat and simmer, covered, until broccoli is tender, about 8 minutes.

Mix milk, flour, and mustard; stir into vegetables. Heat to boiling; boil, stirring constantly, until thickened. Reduce heat to low; stir in sour cream and dill weed and cook 1 to 2 minutes longer. Season to taste with salt and white pepper. Serve over noodles.

WINE-GLAZED RAVIOLI AND ASPARAGUS

A reduction of vegetable broth, white wine, and orange juice creates an elegant and fragrant sauce for flavorful pasta.

1 package (9 ounces) fresh mushroom ravioli
2 cups canned reduced-sodium vegetable broth
1 cup dry white wine
1 cup orange juice
1/4 teaspoon crushed red pepper
1 pound asparagus, cut into 1-inch pieces
2 tablespoons margarine
Salt and pepper, to taste

Cook ravioli according to package directions. While pasta is cooking . . .

Heat vegetable broth, white wine, orange juice, and crushed red pepper to boiling in large skillet; boil, uncovered, 10 minutes or until liquid is reduced to about 1/2 cup.

Add asparagus to skillet; cook, covered, over medium heat until crisp-tender, 3 to 4 minutes. Add ravioli and margarine; season to taste with salt and pepper.

V

PREP/COOK TIME:

20 minutes

SERVINGS: **4**

PER SERVING:
Calories: 290
Protein (g): 8.2
Carbohydrate (g): 33
Fat (g): 10.6
Saturated Fat (g): 3.6
Cholesterol (mg): 26.8
Dietary Fiber (g): 2.4
Sodium (mg): 254

LIGHT SUMMER PASTA

The fragrant aroma and flavor of fresh herbs and garlic accent summer ripe tomatoes in this salad.

PREP/COOK TIME:

15–20 minutes

SERVINGS: *4*

8   ounces spaghetti
1   pound Italian plum tomatoes, chopped
¾   cup (3 ounces) cubed (¼ inch) reduced-fat mozzarella cheese
3   tablespoons finely chopped fresh basil leaves, *or* 2 teaspoons dried
2   tablespoons finely chopped parsley
    Garlic Vinaigrette (recipe follows)

Cook spaghetti according to package directions. Rinse under cold water until cool; drain well.

Combine spaghetti, tomatoes, cheese, and herbs in salad bowl; pour Garlic Vinaigrette over and toss.

GARLIC VINAIGRETTE

makes about ⅓ cup

3   tablespoons red wine vinegar
2   tablespoons olive oil
2   teaspoons minced garlic
¼   teaspoon salt
⅛   teaspoon pepper

PER SERVING:
Calories: 394
Protein (g): 15.8
Carbohydrate (g): 57.2
Fat (g): 11.8
Saturated Fat (g): 3.2
Cholesterol (mg): 10.3
Dietary Fiber (g): 4.5
Sodium (mg): 303

Mix all ingredients.

20-MINUTE RAVIOLI

Use any favorite flavor of refrigerated fresh ravioli with this quick and nutritious bean sauce.

 1 package (9 ounces) fresh sun-dried tomato ravioli
¾ cup chopped onion
 2 teaspoons minced garlic
 1 tablespoon olive oil
¾ cup canned kidney beans, rinsed, drained
 1 large tomato, cubed
½ teaspoon dried thyme leaves
   Salt and pepper, to taste

Cook ravioli according to package directions.

Saute onion and garlic in oil in large skillet until tender, about 5 minutes. Stir in beans, tomato, and thyme; cook 2 to 3 minutes. Stir in ravioli and cook 2 to 3 minutes longer. Season to taste with salt and pepper.

PREP/COOK TIME:

20 minutes

SERVINGS: **4**

PER SERVING:
Calories: 198
Protein (g): 8
Carbohydrate (g): 25.5
Fat (g): 7.6
Saturated Fat (g): 2.7
Cholesterol (mg): 15.4
Dietary Fiber (g): 4.9
Sodium (mg): 336

PASTA AND PORTOBELLO MUSHROOMS VINAIGRETTE

PREP/COOK TIME:

20 minutes

SERVINGS: *4*

For a great picnic or pot-luck dish, make the salad early in the day and allow it to marinate in the refrigerator. Arrange on lettuce at serving time.

8	ounces rotini
12	ounces sliced portobello mushrooms
1	tablespoon olive oil
2	medium tomatoes, cut into wedges
1	medium yellow squash, *or* zucchini, sliced
1	medium green bell pepper, sliced
1	large carrot, sliced
1	small red onion, sliced
½–¾	cup reduced-fat Italian dressing
	Lettuce leaves, for garnish

Cook rotini according to package directions. Rinse under cold water until cool; drain well.

Saute mushrooms in oil in large skillet until tender, 5 to 8 minutes. Combine mushrooms, vegetables, and pasta in bowl; pour Italian dressing over and toss. Arrange lettuce on salad plates; spoon salad over.

PER SERVING:
Calories: 333
Protein (g): 11.4
Carbohydrate (g): 54.3
Fat (g): 9.2
Saturated Fat (g): 1.2
Cholesterol (mg): 1.8
Dietary Fiber (g): 4.9
Sodium (mg): 260

MAFALDE WITH GARBANZO BEANS, FRESH TOMATOES, AND CROUTONS

An easy-to-make dish with many flavor and color contrasts.

L

PREP/COOK TIME:
20 minutes
SERVINGS: 4

8	ounces mafalde, *or* other flat pasta
½	cup chopped poblano chili, *or* green bell pepper
⅓	cup chopped onion
1	teaspoon minced garlic
2	teaspoons olive oil
1	can (15 ounces) garbanzo beans, rinsed, drained
2	cups seeded, chopped Italian plum tomatoes
¼	cup loosely packed basil leaves, chopped
¼	cup reduced-fat Italian salad dressing
1½	cups herb, *or* Parmesan, croutons
	Shredded Parmesan cheese, for garnish

Cook mafalde according to package directions. While pasta is cooking . . .

Saute poblano chili, onion, and garlic in oil in medium skillet until tender, 5 to 8 minutes. Add beans and cook, covered, over medium heat until hot through, 2 to 3 minutes. Remove from heat and stir in tomatoes, basil, and salad dressing.

Toss pasta and bean mixture in serving bowl; add croutons and toss. Serve with Parmesan cheese.

PER SERVING:
Calories: 424
Protein (g): 15.2
Carbohydrate (g): 76.2
Fat (g): 7.1
Saturated Fat (g): 1
Cholesterol (mg): 0.9
Dietary Fiber (g): 9.7
Sodium (mg): 694

BLACK BEAN AND SMOKED TOFU SALAD

PREPARATION TIME:

15–20 minutes

SERVINGS: *6*

(about 1¼ cups each)

The smoky flavor of the tofu is a pleasant contrast to the picante chili, fresh-flavored cilantro, and Mustard-Honey Dressing. Purchased salad dressing may be used.

2 cans (15 ounces each) black beans, rinsed, drained
3 packages (6 ounces each) smoked tofu, cubed
1 large tomato, seeded, chopped
1 medium red, *or* green, bell pepper, chopped
½ cup thinly sliced red onion
¼ cup finely chopped cilantro
¼ cup finely chopped parsley
1 jalapeño chili, finely chopped
2 teaspoons minced roasted garlic
  Mustard-Honey Dressing (recipe follows), *or* ½ cup prepared honey-Dijon dressing
  Lettuce leaves, for garnish

Combine all ingredients, except Mustard-Honey Dressing and lettuce, in salad bowl; pour dressing over and toss. Serve on lettuce-lined plates.

MUSTARD-HONEY DRESSING

makes about ½ cup

2–4 tablespoons olive oil
2–3 tablespoons cider vinegar
1 tablespoon Dijon-style mustard
1–2 tablespoons honey

Mix all ingredients.

PER SERVING:
Calories: 246
Protein (g): 16
Carbohydrate (g): 26.5
Fat (g): 9.7
Saturated Fat (g): 1.1
Cholesterol (mg): 0.1
Dietary Fiber (g): 8.5
Sodium (mg): 522

CREAMY FETTUCCINE PRIMAVERA

The sauce for this dish should be somewhat thin, as it thickens once it is removed from the heat. Purchase your mushrooms and broccoflower already cut to minimize preparation time.

L

PREP/COOK TIME:

20 minutes

SERVINGS: 4

8 ounces fettuccine, *or* linguine

Vegetable cooking spray

2 cups sliced mushrooms

2 cups broccoflower, *or* cauliflower, florets

½ cup chopped red, *or* green, bell pepper

½ cup water

1 package (8 ounces) reduced-fat cream cheese

⅔–1 cup 2% reduced-fat milk, divided

¼ cup sliced green onion and tops

½ teaspoon dried Italian seasoning

2 tablespoons grated Parmesan cheese

Salt and white pepper, to taste

Cook fettuccine according to package directions. While pasta is cooking . . .

Spray large skillet with cooking spray; heat over medium heat until hot. Saute mushrooms, broccoflower, and bell pepper 3 to 4 minutes. Add water and heat to boiling. Reduce heat and simmer, covered, until broccoflower is tender and water absorbed, about 8 minutes.

Heat cream cheese, ⅔ cup milk, green onion, and Italian seasoning in small saucepan over low heat until cream cheese is melted, stirring frequently. Stir in Parmesan cheese and enough remaining milk to make a thin consistency (sauce will thicken when removed from heat). Season to taste with salt and pepper.

Pour sauce over fettuccine in serving bowl and toss; add vegetable mixture and toss gently.

PER SERVING:

Calories: 339
Protein (g): 15.5
Carbohydrate (g): 40.2
Fat (g): 12.7
Saturated Fat (g): 7.2
Cholesterol (mg): 41.6
Dietary Fiber (g): 1.7
Sodium (mg): 353

GREAT GARLIC PASTA

L

PREP/COOK TIME:
15–20 minutes
SERVINGS: **4**

Slow-cooking gives a sweet, mellow flavor to the garlic. Prepared peeled garlic can be found in jars in the produce section of most supermarkets.

8	ounces (2 cups) orrechiette, *or* cappelletti
1	cup tiny peas
⅓	cup slivered (¼-inch pieces), *or* thinly sliced, garlic
2–3	teaspoons olive oil
2	tablespoons minced fresh parsley
1	tablespoon minced fresh rosemary, *or* 1 teaspoon crushed dried rosemary leaves
¼–⅓	cup freshly grated Parmesan cheese
	Salt and pepper, to taste

Cook pasta according to package directions, adding peas 1 minute before end of cooking time; drain. While pasta is cooking . . .

Cook garlic over very low heat in oil in small skillet until very tender but not browned, about 10 minutes. Add herbs; toss with pasta and cheese in serving bowl. Season to taste with salt and pepper.

PER SERVING:
Calories: 302
Protein (g): 12.1
Carbohydrate (g): 52.2
Fat (g): 5
Saturated Fat (g): 1.4
Cholesterol (mg): 3.9
Dietary Fiber (g): 4.5
Sodium (mg): 132

ASPARAGUS AND WHITE BEANS, ITALIAN-STYLE

Imagine yourself in a medieval town in Tuscany while enjoying this spring asparagus and bean saute.

L

PREP/COOK TIME:

15–20 minutes

SERVINGS: *4*

8	ounces linguine, *or* thin spaghetti
1	pound asparagus, cut into 2-inch pieces
2	teaspoons minced garlic
2–3	teaspoons olive oil
2	cups chopped Italian plum tomatoes
1	can (15 ounces) cannellini, *or* Great Northern, beans, rinsed, drained
1	teaspoon dried rosemary leaves, *or* Italian seasoning
1	cup canned reduced-sodium vegetable broth
	Salt and pepper, to taste
¼–½	cup (1–2 ounces) shredded Parmesan cheese

Cook pasta according to package directions. While pasta is cooking . . .

Saute asparagus and garlic in oil in large skillet until crisp-tender, 3 to 4 minutes. Stir in remaining ingredients, except salt, pepper, and cheese. Heat to boiling; reduce heat and simmer rapidly until mixture has thickened, 3 to 5 minutes. Season to taste with salt and pepper.

Serve vegetable mixture over pasta; sprinkle with cheese.

PER SERVING:
Calories: 339
Protein (g): 15.8
Carbohydrate (g): 58.7
Fat (g): 6.1
Saturated Fat (g): 1.4
Cholesterol (mg): 3.9
Dietary Fiber (g): 8.9
Sodium (mg): 458

ITALIAN-STYLE BEANS AND VEGETABLES

PREP/COOK TIME:

20 minutes

SERVINGS: **6**

(about 1¼ cups each)

This colorful vegetable mélange can also be served over pasta, rice, or squares of warm cornbread.

1½ cups chopped onions
1½ cups chopped portobello mushrooms
3–4 tablespoons olive oil, divided
2 cups broccoli florets and sliced stems
1 cup sliced yellow summer squash
1 can (15 ounces) garbanzo beans, rinsed, drained
1 can (15 ounces) red kidney beans, rinsed, drained
1 can (14½ ounces) diced tomatoes with roasted garlic, undrained
1 teaspoon dried basil leaves
¼–½ teaspoon crushed red pepper
Salt and pepper, to taste
1½ packages (16-ounce size) prepared polenta, cut into 12 slices

Saute onions and mushrooms in 2 tablespoons of oil in large saucepan for 5 minutes. Add broccoli and squash; cook, covered, over medium heat 2 to 3 minutes.

Stir in beans, tomatoes with liquid, basil, and crushed red pepper; heat to boiling. Reduce heat and simmer, covered, until broccoli is crisp-tender, 5 to 8 minutes. Season to taste with salt and pepper.

While stew is simmering, saute slices of polenta in large skillet according to package directions, using remaining olive oil as needed. Serve bean mixture over polenta slices.

PER SERVING:
Calories: 353
Protein (g): 13.5
Carbohydrate (g): 52.2
Fat (g): 11.1
Saturated Fat (g): 1.9
Cholesterol (mg): 2.3
Dietary Fiber (g): 12.3
Sodium (mg): 1060

EGGPLANT AND VEGETABLE SAUTE

Minced roasted garlic is available in jars in your produce section; substitute regular minced garlic if desired.

8 ounces whole wheat spaghetti, *or* any desired pasta
1 large eggplant (about 1¼ pounds), unpeeled, cubed (½ inch)
3 cups frozen stir-fry pepper blend
4 teaspoons minced roasted garlic
¾ teaspoon dried rosemary leaves
½ teaspoon dried thyme leaves
2 teaspoons olive oil
1 can (15 ounces) cannellini, *or* Great Northern, beans, rinsed, drained
Salt and pepper, to taste

Cook pasta according to package directions. While pasta is cooking . . .

Cook eggplant, pepper blend, garlic, and herbs in oil in large saucepan over medium heat, covered, until vegetables are tender, 8 to 10 minutes, stirring occasionally. Stir in beans; cook until hot through, 1 to 2 minutes. Season to taste with salt and pepper. Serve eggplant mixture over spaghetti.

PREP/COOK TIME:
20 minutes
SERVINGS: **4**
(about 1 cup each)

PER SERVING:
Calories: 337
Protein (g): 13.6
Carbohydrate (g): 65.8
Fat (g): 3.8
Saturated Fat (g): 0.5
Cholesterol (mg): 0
Dietary Fiber (g): 15.5
Sodium (mg): 241

VEGETABLE CURRY

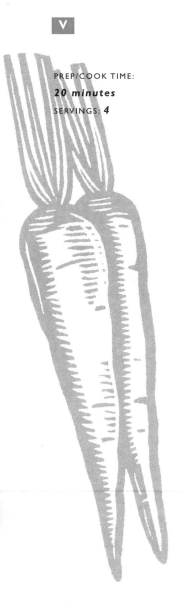

PREP/COOK TIME:

20 minutes

SERVINGS: *4*

A variety of spices and herbs are combined to make the fragrant curry that seasons this dish. One and one-half teaspoons of purchased curry powder may be substituted.

1	package (6¼ ounces) fast-cooking long-grain and wild rice mix
½	cup chopped onion
1	teaspoon minced garlic
	Curry Seasoning (recipe follows)
1	tablespoon vegetable oil
16	ounces cauliflower, *or* broccoli, florets
¼	package (1-pound, 4-ounce size) refrigerated potato wedges
1½	cups baby carrots
1½	cups vegetable broth
1	tablespoon flour
2	tablespoons cold water
1	large tomato, chopped
1–2	tablespoons lemon juice
	Salt, cayenne, and black pepper, to taste

Cook rice according to package directions, discarding spice packet. While rice is cooking . . .

Saute onion, garlic, and Curry Seasoning in oil in large saucepan 2-3 minutes. Add cauliflower, potatoes, carrots, and broth to saucepan; heat to boiling. Reduce heat and simmer, covered, until vegetables are tender, about 8 to 10 minutes.

Heat vegetable mixture to boiling. Mix flour and water; stir into boiling mixture. Cook, stirring constantly, until thickened. Stir in tomato and lemon juice; simmer 2 to 3 minutes longer. Season to taste with salt, cayenne, and black pepper. Serve over rice.

CURRY SEASONING

¾ teaspoon ground turmeric

¼ teaspoon dry mustard

¼ teaspoon ground cumin

¼ teaspoon ground coriander

Mix all ingredients.

PER SERVING:
Calories: 286
Protein (g): 11
Carbohydrate (g): 53.3
Fat (g): 4.3
Saturated Fat (g): 0.5
Cholesterol (mg): 0
Dietary Fiber (g): 7.5
Sodium (mg): 465

THAI FRIED RICE

PREP/COOK TIME:
15–20 minutes
SERVINGS: **2**

Although packaged coconut ginger rice is delicious, any kind of leftover rice can be used, making this speedy dish even faster to prepare!

1	package (6.4 ounces) Thai coconut ginger rice, *or* 1 ½ cups cooked rice
1	package (16 ounces) frozen vegetable stir-fry blend with sugar snap peas
6	green onions and tops, sliced, divided
½–1	teaspoon hot chili sesame oil
2	eggs, lightly beaten
2–3	tablespoons Thai peanut sauce
1–2	tablespoons reduced-sodium tamari sauce

Cook rice according to package directions.

Stir-fry frozen vegetables and 4 green onions in sesame oil in large skillet until tender, 3 to 4 minutes. Move vegetables to side of skillet.

Add eggs to skillet; cook over medium heat until set, stirring occasionally, about 2 minutes. Break up eggs with spatula and mix with vegetables; stir in rice and peanut and tamari sauces.

Spoon rice mixture into serving dish and sprinkle with remaining sliced green onions.

TIP

Mix 1 to 2 tablespoons reduced-fat peanut butter, 2 to 3 teaspoons tamari soy sauce, and ½ to 1 teaspoon minced gingerroot as a substitute for the Thai peanut sauce.

PER SERVING:
Calories: 337
Protein (g): 19.6
Carbohydrate (g): 47.4
Fat (g): 7.6
Saturated Fat (g): 1.9
Cholesterol (mg): 212
Dietary Fiber (g): 4.7
Sodium (mg): 967

THAI STIR-FRY

With a few convenience foods in your pantry, everyday vegetables can be transformed into an exotic meal.

1 package (6.4 ounces) Thai coconut ginger rice
  Oriental-flavored vegetable cooking spray
8 green onions and tops, sliced
8 ounces broccoli florets
8 ounces carrots, thinly sliced
1 cup Thai peanut sauce
½ cup canned reduced-sodium vegetable broth
2 teaspoons cornstarch
¼ cup finely chopped cilantro
¼ cup dry roasted peanuts, optional

Prepare rice according to package directions.

Spray large skillet with cooking spray; heat over medium heat until hot. Saute onions, broccoli, and carrots until crisp-tender, 4 to 5 minutes. Stir in peanut sauce; stir in combined vegetable broth and cornstarch; heat to boiling. Boil until thickened, about 1 minute.

Serve vegetable mixture over rice; sprinkle with cilantro and peanuts.

TIP

An aromatic rice, such as basmati or jasmine, can be substituted for the Thai rice; cook with light coconut milk, if desired, or sprinkle with flaked coconut when serving.

V

PREP/COOK TIME:

20 minutes

SERVINGS: **4**

PER SERVING:
Calories: 238
Protein (g): 10.2
Carbohydrate (g): 38.3
Fat (g): 5.4
Saturated Fat (g): 1
Cholesterol (mg): 0
Dietary Fiber (g): 6.3
Sodium (mg): 1433

SESAME ASPARAGUS STIR-FRY

PREP/COOK TIME:
18–20 minutes
SERVINGS: *4*
(about 1 cup each)

Check the Asian section of your supermarket for the interesting selection of sauces available for noodles and rice.

1 package (18 ounces) Chinese egg noodles Oriental, *or* plain, vegetable cooking spray

8 ounces asparagus, cut into 1-inch pieces

¼ teaspoon dried red pepper flakes

1 can (15 ounces) black beans, rinsed, drained

1 jar (14 ounces) Mandarin sesame sauce for noodles and rice

1 small tomato, coarsely chopped

Cook noodles according to package directions.

Spray wok or medium skillet with cooking spray; heat over medium heat until hot. Stir-fry asparagus 3 to 4 minutes or until browned. Add red pepper flakes; cook 1 minute longer.

Stir beans and Mandarin sesame sauce into skillet and cook 2 to 3 minutes; stir in tomato. Serve over noodles.

PER SERVING:
Calories: 387
Protein (g): 9.3
Carbohydrate (g): 74.6
Fat (g): 6.2
Saturated Fat (g): 0.8
Cholesterol (mg): 0
Dietary Fiber (g): 11.5
Sodium (mg): 1187

MEATLESS SLOPPY JOES

A sandwich for kids of all ages! Serve with lots of pickles and fresh vegetable relishes.

V

PREP/COOK TIME:
20 minutes
SERVINGS: **4**

½ cup chopped onion
½ cup chopped green, *or* red, bell pepper
1 teaspoon minced garlic
1–2 tablespoons vegetable oil
½ cup catsup
⅔ cup water
2 tablespoons light brown sugar
1 tablespoon prepared mustard
½ teaspoon chili powder
⅔ cup textured vegetable protein
Salt and pepper, to taste
4 whole wheat hamburger buns, toasted

Saute onion, bell pepper, and garlic in oil in medium saucepan 5 minutes. Stir in catsup, water, brown sugar, mustard, chili powder, and vegetable protein; heat to boiling. Reduce heat and simmer, covered, 10 minutes. Season to taste with salt and pepper. Spoon sandwich mixture into buns.

PER SERVING:
Calories: 264
Protein (g): 16.3
Carbohydrate (g): 40.1
Fat (g): 5.7
Saturated Fat (g): 0.9
Cholesterol (mg): 0.1
Dietary Fiber (g): 5.5
Sodium (mg): 617

CRANBERRY CHEESE MELT

L

PREP/COOK TIME:
15 minutes
SERVINGS: **4**

Lots of melty cheese, with cranberry and walnut accents.

¼ package (8-ounce size) fat-free cream cheese, softened
¼ cup (1 ounce) shredded smoked Gouda, *or* Swiss, cheese
¼ cup chopped walnuts
8 slices whole wheat bread
½ medium onion, thinly sliced
¼ cup whole-berry cranberry sauce
½ cup (2 ounces) shredded fat-free Cheddar cheese
Butter-flavored vegetable cooking spray

Mix cream cheese, Gouda cheese, and walnuts; spread on 4 slices bread. Arrange onion slices over cheese; top with cranberry sauce, Cheddar cheese, and remaining bread slices.

Spray large skillet with cooking spray; heat over medium heat until hot. Cook sandwiches over medium heat until browned on the bottoms, about 5 minutes. Spray tops of sandwiches with spray and turn; cook until browned on other side, about 5 minutes.

PER SERVING:
Calories: 263
Protein (g): 15.2
Carbohydrate (g): 33.7
Fat (g): 8.7
Saturated Fat (g): 2.1
Cholesterol (mg): 9.2
Dietary Fiber (g): 4.4
Sodium (mg): 504

FALAFEL "BURGERS"

The falafel mixture can also be shaped into 1-inch balls and cooked as the package directs. Serve with Yogurt Cucumber Sauce as appetizers, or in pitas for sandwiches.

L

PREP/COOK TIME:
20 minutes
SERVINGS: *4*
(2 "burgers" each)

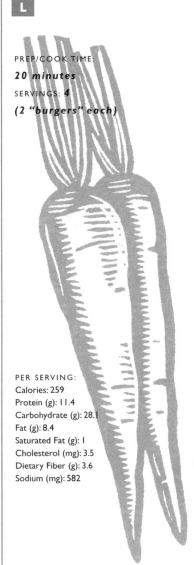

  1 package (6 ounces) falafel mix
 ½ cup shredded carrots
 ¼ cup sunflower kernels
  2 tablespoons thinly sliced green onions and tops
     Vegetable cooking spray
     Yogurt Cucumber Sauce (recipe follows)

Prepare falafel mix with water according to package directions; mix in carrots, sunflower kernels, and green onions. Shape mixture into 8 "burgers" about ½ inch thick.

Spray large skillet with cooking spray; heat over medium heat until hot. Place "burgers" in skillet and spray tops with cooking spray. Cook patties until browned, 4 to 5 minutes on each side.

Make Yogurt Cucumber Sauce while "burgers" are cooking; serve with "burgers."

YOGURT CUCUMBER SAUCE

makes about 1⅓ cups

  1 cup reduced-fat plain yogurt
  1 cup shredded, *or* chopped, cucumber
 ½ teaspoon dried dill weed
 ½ teaspoon dried mint leaves
     Salt and white pepper, to taste

Mix yogurt, cucumber, and herbs. Season to taste with salt and pepper.

PER SERVING:
Calories: 259
Protein (g): 11.4
Carbohydrate (g): 28.1
Fat (g): 8.4
Saturated Fat (g): 1
Cholesterol (mg): 3.5
Dietary Fiber (g): 3.6
Sodium (mg): 582

MESQUITE HASH AND EGGS

PREP/COOK TIME:
20 minutes
SERVINGS: **4**

You'll enjoy the unusual smoky mesquite flavor of this vegetable hash.

Mesquite-flavor vegetable cooking spray
1   cup chopped onions
1/2   package (16-ounce size) refrigerated cubed potatoes
1   cup frozen peas
1   cup fresh, *or* canned, drained whole-kernel corn
1/4 – 1/2   teaspoon dried thyme leaves
Salt and pepper, to taste
4   eggs

Spray large skillet with cooking spray; heat over medium heat until hot. Saute onions 2 minutes; add potatoes and spray generously with cooking spray. Cook over medium heat until potatoes are browned, about 8 to 10 minutes, stirring frequently. Add peas, corn, and thyme; cook 2 to 3 minutes longer. Season to taste with salt and pepper.

Move hash to sides of skillet; add eggs to center of skillet. Cook, sunny side up, covered, over low heat until eggs are done, 3 to 4 minutes; season to taste with salt and pepper.

PER SERVING:
Calories: 203
Protein (g): 11
Carbohydrate (g): 29.3
Fat (g): 5.4
Saturated Fat (g): 1.6
Cholesterol (mg): 212
Dietary Fiber (g): 4.7
Sodium (mg): 103

SWEET POTATO HASH AND EGGS

A colorful hash dish that's perfect for a hearty breakfast, brunch, or light supper.

2	cups cubed (½ inch), peeled sweet potatoes
2	cups cubed (½ inch), unpeeled Idaho potatoes
½	cup chopped onion
½	cup chopped red, *or* green, bell pepper
1	teaspoon dried rosemary leaves
½	teaspoon dried thyme leaves
1–2	tablespoons margarine
	Salt and pepper, to taste
4	eggs

Cook vegetables and herbs in margarine in large skillet, covered, over medium heat 10 minutes. Uncover and cook over medium-high heat until vegetables are browned and tender, about 5 minutes, stirring occasionally. Season to taste with salt and pepper.

While potatoes are cooking, fry eggs in lightly greased medium skillet over medium heat. Spoon hash onto plates; top each serving with an egg.

PREP/COOK TIME:
20 minutes
SERVINGS: **4**

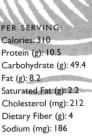

PER SERVING:
Calories: 310
Protein (g): 10.5
Carbohydrate (g): 49.4
Fat (g): 8.2
Saturated Fat (g): 2.2
Cholesterol (mg): 212
Dietary Fiber (g): 4
Sodium (mg): 186

BREAKFAST BURRITOS

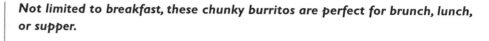

LO

Not limited to breakfast, these chunky burritos are perfect for brunch, lunch, or supper.

PREP/COOK TIME:
20 minutes
SERVINGS: **6**
(1 burrito each)

1	package (1 pound, 4 ounces) refrigerated potato wedges
1½	cups cubed zucchini
1	cup chopped red, *or* green, bell peppers
½	cup sliced green onions and tops
2	teaspoons minced garlic
1	tablespoon margarine
8	eggs, lightly beaten
¾	teaspoon dried oregano leaves
	Salt and pepper, to taste
6	flour tortillas (10 inch)
1	cup (4 ounces) shredded reduced-fat mozzarella, *or* Cheddar, cheese
1½	cups mild, *or* hot, salsa

Saute potatoes, zucchini, bell peppers, green onions, and garlic in margarine in large skillet until potatoes are browned and peppers and onions are tender, about 10 minutes.

Add eggs and oregano to skillet and cook until eggs are set, stirring occasionally. Season to taste with salt and pepper.

Spoon mixture onto tortillas; sprinkle with cheese. Fold two sides of each tortilla in about 2 inches, then roll up from other side to enclose filling. Serve with salsa.

PER SERVING:
Calories: 363
Protein (g): 22.5
Carbohydrate (g): 40
Fat (g): 14.5
Saturated Fat (g): 4.8
Cholesterol (mg): 292.7
Dietary Fiber (g): 4
Sodium (mg): 929

VERY BERRY SMOOTHIE

Perfect for breakfast, lunch, or a substantial snack when you need a pick-me-up! Nutrition-packed, beans are a valuable source of folate, banana a high source of potassium.

1½ cups orange juice
1 can (15 ounces) Great Northern, *or* navy, beans, rinsed, drained
1 cup frozen, *or* fresh, hulled strawberries
1 cup frozen, *or* fresh, blueberries
1 small banana
2–3 tablespoons honey
1½ teaspoons ground cinnamon
⅛ teaspoon ground nutmeg
6–8 ice cubes

Process all ingredients, except ice cubes, in blender until smooth. Add ice cubes and blend until smooth. If a thinner consistency is desired, stir in additional orange juice or water. Serve in glasses.

TIP

Berry Smoothies can be made 1 to 2 days in advance; refrigerate, covered. The drink will thicken in the refrigerator; stir in orange juice or cold water to make desired consistency.

V

PREPARATION TIME:
10 minutes
SERVINGS: 4
(about 8 ounces each)

PER SERVING:
Calories: 192
Protein (g): 6.4
Carbohydrate (g): 47.3
Fat (g): 0.8
Saturated Fat (g): 0.1
Cholesterol (mg): 0
Dietary Fiber (g): 8.5
Sodium (mg): 413

TOFRUITY

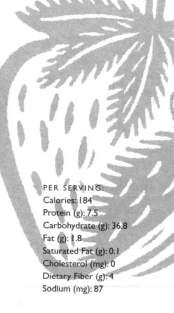

PREPARATION TIME:

10 minutes

SERVINGS: *2*

(about 1 1/2 cups each)

A light yet nutritious meal on the go, ready when you are! Make it up to 24 hours in advance for convenience, then shake or stir before serving.

1/2 package (14-ounce size) light silken tofu, drained
1 cup cubed, pitted, peeled mango
3/4 cup frozen strawberries, *or* raspberries
1–1 1/2 cups orange juice

Process all ingredients in blender or food processor until smooth, adding enough orange juice to make desired consistency. Serve in tall glasses.

PER SERVING:
Calories: 184
Protein (g): 7.5
Carbohydrate (g): 36.8
Fat (g): 1.8
Saturated Fat (g): 0.1
Cholesterol (mg): 0
Dietary Fiber (g): 4
Sodium (mg): 87

one-dish dinners

Vegetables Marengo

Winter Bean and Vegetable Stew

Cabbage Ragout with Mashed Potatoes

Veggie Stew with Dumplings

Bean and Squash Stew

Baked Fusilli and Cheese Primavera

Vegetable and Mixed Rice Casserole

Goat's Cheese and Vegetable Casserole

Autumn Pot Pie

Veggie Pie

Veggie Shepherd's Pie

Vegetarian Tetrazzini

VEGETABLES MARENGO

A delicious dish that picks up the colors and flavors of the Mediterranean.

1 package (10½ ounces) light tofu, cut into scant 1-inch cubes
2 tablespoons olive oil
2 medium onions, cut into wedges
2 medium zucchini, cubed
1 cup small mushrooms
1 teaspoon minced garlic
1 tablespoon flour
1 can (14½ ounces) diced tomatoes, undrained
¾ cup vegetable broth
1 strip orange rind (3 x 1 inch)
½ teaspoon dried thyme leaves
½ teaspoon dried oregano leaves
  Salt and pepper, to taste
3 cups cooked couscous, *or* rice, warm

PREPARATION TIME:
10–15 minutes
COOKING TIME:
25–30 minutes
SERVINGS: **4**
(about 1¼ cups each)

Cook tofu in oil in large saucepan over medium heat until browned on all sides, about 5 minutes. Remove from saucepan and reserve.

Add onions, zucchini, mushrooms, and garlic to saucepan; saute 5 minutes. Stir in flour and cook 1 to 2 minutes longer. Add tomatoes, broth, orange rind, herbs, and reserved tofu; heat to boiling. Reduce heat and simmer, covered, until vegetables are tender, 10 to 15 minutes. Season to taste with salt and pepper. Serve mixture over couscous in shallow bowls.

PER SERVING:
Calories: 310
Protein (g): 13.1
Carbohydrate (g): 46.6
Fat (g): 8.5
Saturated Fat (g): 1
Cholesterol (mg): 0
Dietary Fiber (g): 5.3
Sodium (mg): 517

WINTER BEAN AND VEGETABLE STEW

Root vegetables and beans combine in this satisfying stew, perfect for cold-weather meals. Serve with crusty Italian bread.

PREPARATION TIME:
20 minutes

COOKING TIME:
25–30 minutes

SERVINGS: **6**

(about 1¹/₃ cups each)

PER SERVING:
Calories: 222
Protein (g): 9.6
Carbohydrate (g): 36.3
Fat (g): 5.6
Saturated Fat (g): 0.7
Cholesterol (mg): 0
Dietary Fiber (g): 9.4
Sodium (mg): 802

1	cup chopped onions
1	medium Idaho potato, unpeeled, cut into 1-inch cubes
1	large sweet potato, peeled, cut into 1-inch cubes
¾	cup chopped green bell pepper
1	teaspoon minced garlic
2	tablespoons olive oil
1	tablespoon flour
1½	cups vegetable broth
1	can (15 ounces) black beans, rinsed, drained
1	can (13¼ ounces) baby lima beans, rinsed, drained
1	can (16 ounces) tomato wedges, undrained
¾	teaspoon dried sage leaves
	Salt and pepper, to taste

Saute onions, potatoes, bell pepper, and garlic in oil in large saucepan 5 minutes; stir in flour and cook 1 to 2 minutes longer.

Add remaining ingredients, except salt and pepper, to saucepan; heat to boiling. Reduce heat and simmer, covered, until vegetables are tender, 15 to 20 minutes. Season to taste with salt and pepper.

CABBAGE RAGOUT WITH MASHED POTATOES

Fresh fennel, gingerroot and apple lend aromatic flavor highlights to this cabbage stew. If fresh fennel is not available, substitute celery and increase the amount of fennel seeds to 1 1/2 teaspoons.

L

PREP/COOK TIME:

35–40 minutes

SERVINGS: **6**

(about 1 1/3 cups each)

1	medium eggplant (about 1 1/4 pounds), unpeeled, cut into 1/2-inch cubes
1	cup chopped onion
1/2	cup thinly sliced fennel bulb
2	teaspoons minced garlic
4	teaspoons minced gingerroot
1	teaspoon fennel seeds, crushed
1–2	tablespoons vegetable oil
8	cups thinly sliced cabbage
2	cups vegetable broth
2	medium apples, cored, cubed
1	cup reduced-fat sour cream
	Salt and pepper, to taste
3/4	package (22-ounce size) frozen mashed potatoes

Saute eggplant, onion, fennel, garlic, gingerroot, and fennel seeds in oil in large saucepan until vegetables are tender and beginning to brown, about 10 minutes, stirring occasionally.

Add cabbage and broth; heat to boiling. Reduce heat and simmer, covered, until cabbage is wilted and crisp-tender, about 5 minutes. Stir apples into cabbage mixture; cook, covered, until apples are tender, about 5 minutes. Stir in sour cream; cook over medium heat until hot through, 3 to 4 minutes. Season to taste with salt and pepper.

While ragout is cooking, prepare mashed potatoes according to package directions. Serve ragout over potatoes.

TIP

You can substitute 1 1/2 packages (16-ounce size) of cabbage slaw mix for the 8 cups of sliced cabbage.

PER SERVING:
Calories: 250
Protein (g): 7.3
Carbohydrate (g): 38.2
Fat (g): 9.2
Saturated Fat (g): 3.5
Cholesterol (mg): 13.5
Dietary Fiber (g): 7.3
Sodium (mg): 512

VEGGIE STEW WITH DUMPLINGS

PREPARATION TIME:

15 minutes

COOKING TIME:

30 minutes

SERVINGS: *6*

(about 1½ cups each)

Dumplings, soft, fluffy, and seasoned with herbs, are an easy topping for this colorful stew. The stew can be made without the dumplings too; serve with freshly baked biscuits instead.

1 cup coarsely chopped onion

1 large red, *or* green, bell pepper, sliced

1 tablespoon vegetable oil

3⅔ cups vegetable broth, divided

3 medium potatoes, unpeeled, cut into ½-inch cubes

2 cups cubed (½ inch), peeled, seeded butternut, *or* acorn, squash

1 medium zucchini, sliced

4 ounces small cremini, *or* white, mushrooms

¾ cup frozen peas

1 teaspoon dried basil leaves

½ teaspoon dried oregano leaves

⅓ cup all-purpose flour

Salt and pepper, to taste

Herb Dumplings (recipe follows)

Saute onion and bell pepper in oil in large saucepan 5 minutes. Stir in 3 cups broth and remaining ingredients except flour, salt and pepper, and Herb Dumplings; heat to boiling. Mix remaining ⅔ cup broth and flour; stir into boiling mixture. Boil, stirring constantly, until thickened, about 1 minute. Reduce heat and simmer, covered, 5 minutes. Season to taste with salt and pepper.

Spoon dumpling mixture on top of stew in 6 large spoonfuls; cook over low heat, uncovered, 10 minutes. Cook, covered, 10 minutes longer or until dumplings are tender and toothpick inserted in center comes out clean. Serve in bowls.

HERB DUMPLINGS

makes 6

 2 cups reduced-fat baking mix
 ½ teaspoon dried basil leaves
 ¼ teaspoon dried oregano leaves
 ⅔ cup 2% reduced-fat milk

Combine baking mix and herbs in small bowl; stir in milk to form soft dough.

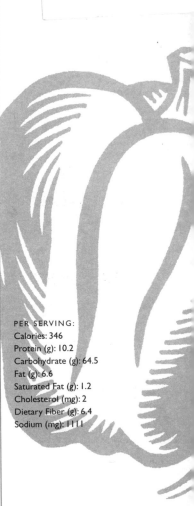

PER SERVING:
Calories: 346
Protein (g): 10.2
Carbohydrate (g): 64.5
Fat (g): 6.6
Saturated Fat (g): 1.2
Cholesterol (mg): 2
Dietary Fiber (g): 6.4
Sodium (mg): 1111

BEAN AND SQUASH STEW

PREPARATION TIME:
15 minutes
COOKING TIME:
15–20 minutes
SERVINGS: *6*
(about 1¼ cups each)

Stews don't have to be long cooked to be good—this delicious stew is simmered to savory goodness in less than 30 minutes. Serve with warm garlic bread.

1½ cups chopped onions
1½ cups chopped green bell peppers
   2 teaspoons minced roasted garlic
1–2 tablespoons vegetable oil
   1 tablespoon flour
   2 cups cubed (½ inch), peeled, seeded butternut, *or* acorn, squash
   2 cans (16 ounces each) diced tomatoes, undrained
   1 can (15 ounces) red kidney beans, rinsed, drained
   1 can (13¼ ounces) baby lima beans, rinsed, drained
½–¾ teaspoon dried Italian seasoning
      Salt and pepper, to taste

Saute onions, bell peppers, and garlic in oil in large saucepan 5 minutes. Stir in flour; cook 1 minute longer.

Add remaining ingredients, except salt and pepper, to saucepan; heat to boiling. Reduce heat and simmer, until vegetables are tender, 10 to 15 minutes. Season to taste with salt and pepper.

PER SERVING:
Calories: 213
Protein (g): 9.9
Carbohydrate (g): 39.5
Fat (g): 2.9
Saturated Fat (g): 0.4
Cholesterol (mg): 0
Dietary Fiber (g): 11.7
Sodium (mg): 834

BAKED FUSILLI AND CHEESE PRIMAVERA

Asparagus spears, broccoli florets, sliced zucchini, carrots, and mushrooms are other vegetable choices for this cheesy casserole.

10 ounces fusilli, *or* rotini
1 cup sliced cremini, *or* white, mushrooms
¾ cup chopped onion
½ cup chopped red, *or* green, bell pepper
1 teaspoon minced garlic
2 tablespoons margarine
3 cups non-fat milk
⅓ cup all-purpose flour
3 ounces light pasteurized process cheese product, cubed
½ cup (2 ounces) shredded reduced-fat sharp, *or* mild, Cheddar cheese
1 teaspoon Dijon-style mustard
¾ cup frozen peas
Salt and pepper, to taste
2 tablespoons unseasoned dry bread crumbs

Cook fusilli according to package directions.

Saute mushrooms, onion, bell pepper, and garlic in margarine in large saucepan until tender, 5 to 8 minutes. Mix milk and flour until blended; stir into saucepan and heat to boiling, stirring constantly. Boil, stirring constantly, until thickened, about 1 minute.

Reduce heat to low; stir in cheeses and mustard, stirring until cheeses are melted. Combine sauce mixture, fusilli, and peas in 2-quart casserole; season to taste with salt and pepper. Sprinkle with bread crumbs. Bake, uncovered, at 375 degrees until bubbly, 20 to 25 minutes.

L

PREP/COOK TIME:
15–20 minutes
BAKING TIME:
20–25 minutes
SERVINGS: *6*
(about 1½ cups each)

PER SERVING:
Calories: 372
Protein (g): 18.2
Carbohydrate (g): 55.8
Fat (g): 8.6
Saturated Fat (g): 3.1
Cholesterol (mg): 14
Dietary Fiber (g): 3.6
Sodium (mg): 482

VEGETABLE AND MIXED RICE CASSEROLE

L

PREP/COOK TIME:
15 minutes

BAKING TIME:
30 minutes

SERVINGS: **6**
(about 1⅓ cups each)

PER SERVING:
Calories: 334
Protein (g): 15.2
Carbohydrate (g): 55
Fat (g): 6.9
Saturated Fat (g): 1.8
Cholesterol (mg): 12.8
Dietary Fiber (g): 6.5
Sodium (mg): 940

Fast-cooking rice is a kitchen lifesaver when minutes count; any preferred rice can be substituted, however.

1	package (6¼ ounces) fast-cooking long-grain and wild rice
1½	cups sliced shiitake, *or* cremini, mushrooms
1	cup sliced zucchini
½	cup chopped onion
½	cup chopped green bell pepper
½	cup chopped red, *or* green, bell pepper
1	teaspoon dried thyme leaves
1–2	tablespoons vegetable oil
1	can (15 ounces) pinto beans, rinsed, drained
1	cup frozen, *or* canned, drained whole-kernel corn
1	cup fat-free sour cream
1	cup (4 ounces) shredded reduced-fat Cheddar cheese, divided
	Salt and pepper, to taste

Cook rice with spice packet according to package direction.

Cook mushrooms, zucchini, onion, bell pepper, and thyme in oil in medium skillet, covered, over medium heat until vegetables are tender, 8 to 10 minutes.

Combine rice, cooked vegetable mixture, beans, corn, sour cream, and ½ cup cheese; season to taste with salt and pepper. Spoon mixture into 2-quart casserole; sprinkle with remaining ½ cup cheese.

Bake, uncovered, at 350 degrees until hot through, about 30 minutes.

GOAT'S CHEESE AND VEGETABLE CASSEROLE

Delicious, with a generous amount of melty cheese.

1½	cups cut asparagus (1½ inch)
1	package (9 ounces) frozen artichoke hearts
1	package (6¼ ounces) fast-cooking long-grain and wild rice
3	ounces fat-free cream cheese, cubed
¾	cup (3 ounces) shredded reduced-fat mozzarella cheese
3–4	ounces goat's cheese, crumbled
	Salt and pepper, to taste

Cook asparagus and artichoke hearts in boiling water to cover 4 minutes. Drain well.

Cook rice with spice packet according to package directions. Mix rice, vegetables, and cheeses; season to taste with salt and pepper. Spoon into 1½-quart casserole.

Bake, covered, at 375 degrees until casserole is hot and cheese is melted, 20 to 30 minutes.

L

PREP/COOK TIME:
15 minutes
BAKING TIME:
20–30 minutes
SERVINGS: *4*
(about 1¼ cups each)

PER SERVING:
Calories: 359
Protein (g): 22.5
Carbohydrate (g): 44
Fat (g): 12.2
Saturated Fat (g): 6.9
Cholesterol (mg): 33.7
Dietary Fiber (g): 6.1
Sodium (mg): 1101

AUTUMN POT PIE

PREP/COOK TIME:

20 minutes

BAKING TIME:

20 minutes

SERVINGS: *4*

(about 1¼ cups each)

PER SERVING:
Calories: 384
Protein (g): 8.7
Carbohydrate (g): 58.4
Fat (g): 15
Saturated Fat (g): 6.1
Cholesterol (mg): 10
Dietary Fiber (g): 5.9
Sodium (mg): 822

Choose ingredients from your garden or produce market for this savory pie.

Olive oil cooking spray
1½ cups frozen stir-fry pepper blend
2 teaspoons minced garlic
¾ teaspoon dried sage leaves
2 pinches ground nutmeg
2 cups vegetable broth
2 medium sweet potatoes, peeled, cubed (½ inch)
1 cup cubed (½ inch), peeled turnip, *or* parsnip
1 cup halved Brussels sprouts
½ cup frozen, *or* canned, drained, baby lima beans
3 tablespoons flour
⅓ cup cold water
Salt and pepper, to taste
1 refrigerated pastry for 9-inch pie

Spray large saucepan with cooking spray; heat over medium heat until hot. Saute pepper blend and garlic until tender, about 5 minutes; stir in sage and nutmeg and cook 1 to 2 minutes longer. Add broth and remaining vegetables; heat to boiling. Reduce heat and simmer, covered, until vegetables are tender, about 10 minutes.

Heat vegetable mixture to boiling. Mix flour and cold water; stir into boiling mixture. Boil, stirring constantly, until thickened. Season to taste with salt and pepper. Pour mixture into 1½-quart casserole or soufflé dish.

Place pastry on top of casserole; fold edge of pastry under and flute or press with tines of fork. Bake pie at 425 degrees until pastry is browned, about 20 minutes. Cool on wire rack 5 minutes before serving.

VEGGIE PIE

This low-fat version of a family favorite is topped with toasted bread crumbs.

Vegetable cooking spray
1 cup sliced leek (white part only)
1 large red, *or* green, bell pepper, sliced
2 teaspoons minced garlic
1½ teaspoons bouquet garni
2 cups vegetable broth
2 medium russet potatoes, peeled, cubed
2 medium yellow summer squash, sliced
1 cup halved green beans
½ cup cauliflower florets
½ cup frozen peas
3 tablespoons flour
⅓ cup cold water
Salt and pepper, to taste
¾ cup fresh bread crumbs
2 tablespoons margarine, melted

PREPARATION TIME:
20 minutes
BAKING TIME:
20 minutes
SERVINGS: **4**
(about 1¼ cups each)

PER SERVING:
Calories: 229
Protein (g): 6.9
Carbohydrate (g): 36.9
Fat (g): 7
Saturated Fat (g): 1.3
Cholesterol (mg): 0
Dietary Fiber (g): 5.8
Sodium (mg): 654

Spray large saucepan with cooking spray; heat over medium heat until hot. Saute leek, bell pepper, and garlic 5 minutes; stir in bouquet garni and cook 1 minute longer. Add broth and remaining vegetables; heat to boiling. Reduce heat and simmer, covered, until vegetables are tender, about 10 minutes.

Heat vegetable mixture to boiling. Mix flour and cold water; stir into boiling mixture. Boil, stirring constantly, until thickened. Season to taste with salt and pepper. Pour mixture into 1½-quart soufflé dish or casserole.

Toss breadcrumbs with margarine; sprinkle over top of casserole. Bake pie at 425 degrees until crumbs are browned, about 20 minutes. Cool on wire rack 5 minutes before serving.

VEGGIE SHEPHERD'S PIE

Topped with traditional mashed potatoes, this comfort food is sure to please.

PREP/COOK TIME:
20 minutes

BAKING TIME:
20 minutes

SERVINGS: **4**
(about 1 1/4 cups each)

Vegetable cooking spray
1 1/2 cups frozen onion seasoning blend
1/2 cup sliced celery
1 teaspoon minced garlic
3/4 teaspoon dried savory leaves
2 cups vegetable broth
1 cup thinly sliced cabbage
1 cup sliced carrots
2 medium Idaho potatoes, unpeeled, cubed
3/4 cup sliced mushrooms
3/4 package (22-ounce size) frozen mashed potatoes
3 tablespoons flour
1/3 cup cold water
Salt and pepper, to taste

Spray large saucepan with cooking spray; heat over medium heat until hot. Saute onion seasoning blend, celery, garlic, and savory 5 minutes. Stir in broth and remaining vegetables (except frozen mashed potatoes) and heat to boiling; reduce heat and simmer, covered, until vegetables are tender, about 10 minutes.

Make mashed potatoes according to package directions.

Heat vegetable mixture to boiling. Mix flour and cold water; stir into boiling mixture. Boil, stirring constantly, until thickened. Season to taste with salt and pepper. Pour mixture into 1 1/2-quart soufflé dish or casserole.

Spoon or pipe mashed potatoes around edge of casserole. Bake at 375 degrees until potatoes are lightly browned, about 20 minutes.

PER SERVING:
Calories: 250
Protein (g): 6.4
Carbohydrate (g): 47.8
Fat (g): 4.7
Saturated Fat (g): 0.7
Cholesterol (mg): 0.3
Dietary Fiber (g): 4.8
Sodium (mg): 737

VEGETARIAN TETRAZZINI

A versatile dish—use any vegetable or pasta you care to substitute.

16 ounces thin spaghetti
8 ounces sliced mushrooms
1 medium zucchini, sliced
1 cup broccoli florets
1 cup sliced red, *or* green, bell pepper
½ cup chopped onion
1–2 tablespoons margarine
2 tablespoons flour
1¾ cups vegetable broth
1 cup non-fat milk
½ cup dry white wine, *or* non-fat milk
¼ cup grated Parmesan cheese
¼ teaspoon ground nutmeg
Salt and pepper, to taste

Cook spaghetti according to package directions; drain.

Saute vegetables in margarine in large saucepan 5 minutes. Sprinkle vegetables with flour and cook 1 to 2 minutes longer. Add broth, milk, and wine; heat to boiling. Boil, stirring constantly, until thickened, about 1 minute (sauce will be very thin).

Stir pasta, Parmesan cheese, and nutmeg into sauce; season to taste with salt and pepper.

Spoon pasta mixture into 2-quart casserole or baking dish. Bake, uncovered, at 375 degrees until lightly browned and bubbly, about 30 minutes.

L

PREP/COOK TIME:
15 minutes
BAKING TIME:
30 minutes
SERVINGS: *8*

PER SERVING:
Calories: 326
Protein (g): 12.8
Carbohydrate (g): 57.3
Fat (g): 4.3
Saturated Fat (g): 1.1
Cholesterol (mg): 2.5
Dietary Fiber (g): 4.2
Sodium (mg): 305

pasta
pronto

Linguine with Fennel and Sun-Dried Tomato Pesto

Pasta Peperonata

Ziti with Gremolata

Pasta from Pescia

Pasta with Greens, Raisins, and Pine Nuts

Bucatini with Brussels Sprouts and Walnuts

Mafalde with Sweet Potatoes and Kale

Tagliatelle with Chili-Mushroom Stroganoff Sauce

Curried Tortellini with Green Beans and Squash

Chinese Noodles with Sweet Potatoes and Snow Peas

Pasta with Goat's Cheese and Onion Confit

Stir-Fried Rice Noodles with Vegetables

LINGUINE WITH FENNEL AND SUN-DRIED TOMATO PESTO

Fennel, or anise, lends a fragrant flavor to this light pasta entrée.

L

PREPARATION TIME:
20–25 minutes
COOKING TIME:
15–20 minutes
SERVINGS: **6**

1	cup thinly sliced onion
1	fennel bulb, thinly sliced
1–2	tablespoons olive oil
1/4	cup dry white wine, *or* water
	Sun-Dried Tomato Pesto (recipe follows)
12	ounces linguine, *or* angel hair pasta, cooked, warm
	Salt and pepper, to taste

Saute onion and fennel in oil in large skillet 2 to 3 minutes. Cook, covered, over medium-low heat until onions are very soft, 10 to 15 minutes. Stir in wine and simmer, covered, 15 to 20 minutes or until wine is almost gone and fennel is tender.

While vegetables are cooking, make Sun-Dried Tomato Pesto.

Spoon onion mixture and Sun-Dried Tomato Pesto over pasta in serving bowl and toss. Season to taste with salt and pepper.

SUN-DRIED TOMATO PESTO

makes 1 1/2 cups

1/2	cup sun-dried tomatoes (not in oil)
1/2	cup very hot water
1/2	cup packed basil leaves
1	teaspoon minced garlic
3–4	tablespoons olive oil
2	tablespoons grated fat-free Parmesan cheese
	Salt and pepper, to taste

Soak tomatoes in hot water in bowl until softened, 5 to 10 minutes. Drain, reserving liquid.

Process tomatoes, basil, garlic, oil, and cheese in food processor or blender, adding enough reserved liquid to make a smooth, spoonable paste. Season to taste with salt and pepper. Serve at room temperature.

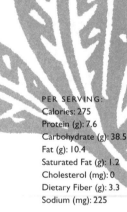

PER SERVING:
Calories: 275
Protein (g): 7.6
Carbohydrate (g): 38.5
Fat (g): 10.4
Saturated Fat (g): 1.2
Cholesterol (mg): 0
Dietary Fiber (g): 3.3
Sodium (mg): 225

PASTA PEPERONATA

Italian peperonata, a slow-cooked mixture of sweet bell peppers, onions, and garlic, is also wonderful served in pita breads.

L

5 large bell peppers, assorted colors, sliced
4 medium onions, sliced
4 teaspoons minced garlic
3 tablespoons olive oil
3 tablespoons water
1 teaspoon sugar
  Salt and pepper, to taste
8 ounces spaghetti, cooked, warm
1/4 cup shredded Parmesan cheese

Saute peppers, onions, and garlic in oil in large skillet 2 to 3 minutes. Add water; cook, covered, over medium to medium-high heat 2 to 3 minutes.

Stir sugar into pepper's mixture; cook, uncovered, over medium-low heat until mixture is very soft and browned, about 20 minutes. Season to taste with salt and pepper. Toss with spaghetti and sprinkle with cheese.

PREPARATION TIME:
15–20 minutes
COOKING TIME:
20 minutes
SERVINGS: *4*

PER SERVING:
Calories: 441
Protein (g): 12.9
Carbohydrate (g): 68.6
Fat (g): 13.2
Saturated Fat (g): 2.5
Cholesterol (mg): 3.9
Dietary Fiber (g): 6.9
Sodium (mg): 101

ZITI WITH GREMOLATA

PREPARATION TIME:
10–15 minutes

COOKING TIME:
15 minutes

SERVINGS: *8*

PER SERVING:
Calories: 254
Protein (g): 8.9
Carbohydrate (g): 52.5
Fat (g): 1.1
Saturated Fat (g): 0.2
Cholesterol (mg): 0
Dietary Fiber (g): 3.4
Sodium (mg): 517

The fresh lemon flavor of the gremolata accents this tomato and pasta dish. Serve with garlic bread and a robust red wine.

Olive oil cooking spray
½ cup chopped onion
8 ounces shiitake, *or* cremini, mushrooms, sliced
2 cans (14½ ounces each) diced tomatoes with Italian seasoning, undrained
Salt and pepper, to taste
1 pound ziti, *or* penne, cooked, warm
Gremolata (recipe follows)

Spray large skillet with cooking spray; heat over medium heat until hot. Saute onion and mushrooms until tender, 5 to 8 minutes. Add tomatoes and heat to boiling; reduce heat and simmer, uncovered, until thickened, about 10 minutes. Season to taste with salt and pepper.

Toss pasta with tomato mixture and half the Gremolata; pass remaining Gremolata to be added as desired.

GREMOLATA

makes about ½ cup

1 cup packed parsley leaves
1–2 teaspoons grated lemon rind
4 large cloves garlic

Process all ingredients in food processor until finely minced, using pulse technique. Refrigerate until serving time.

PASTA FROM PESCIA

I have fond memories of this hearty dish from the Tuscany region of Italy. To save preparation time, use cabbage slaw mix to replace the sliced cabbage in the recipe.

L

PREPARATION TIME:
15–20 minutes
COOKING TIME:
10–15 minutes
SERVINGS: *4*

8	small new potatoes (1 pound), unpeeled
3	cups thinly sliced cabbage
1½	cups halved Brussels sprouts
2	medium carrots, diagonally sliced
1	teaspoon minced garlic
½	teaspoon dried sage leaves
⅓	cup vegetable broth
⅓	cup shredded Parmesan cheese
1	tablespoon minced parsley
	Salt and pepper, to taste
8	ounces rigatoni, *or* ziti, cooked, warm

Cook potatoes in 2 inches simmering water until tender, about 10 minutes; drain. Heat cabbage, Brussels sprouts, carrots, garlic, sage, and broth to boiling in large skillet. Reduce heat and simmer, covered, until cabbage is wilted, about 5 minutes. Add potatoes and cook, uncovered, until liquid is gone and cabbage is lightly browned, about 5 minutes.

Stir cheese and parsley into vegetables; season to taste with salt and pepper. Spoon mixture over pasta on serving platter and toss.

PER SERVING:
Calories: 401
Protein (g): 15.9
Carbohydrate (g): 78.8
Fat (g): 3.6
Saturated Fat (g): 1.5
Cholesterol (mg): 5.2
Dietary Fiber (g): 9.3
Sodium (mg): 256

PASTA WITH GREENS, RAISINS, AND PINE NUTS

V

PREPARATION TIME:
15–20 minutes
COOKING TIME:
20–25 minutes
SERVINGS: **4**

Radicchio, escarole, curly endive, or mustard greens can be substituted for the kale in this sweet-and-bitter Italian favorite.

3–4	medium onions, sliced
2	teaspoons minced garlic
1	tablespoon olive oil
1	teaspoon sugar
12	ounces kale leaves, sliced
1/3	cup dark raisins
1/2	cup vegetable broth
	Salt and pepper, to taste
8	ounces spaghetti, *or* linguine, cooked, warm
1/4	cup pine nuts, *or* slivered almonds

Saute onions and garlic in oil in large skillet 5 minutes. Stir in sugar; cook over low heat until onions are golden, 10 to 15 minutes, stirring occasionally.

Stir kale, raisins, and broth into onion mixture; cook, covered, over low heat until kale is wilted, about 10 minutes. Season to taste with salt and pepper. Spoon mixture over spaghetti and toss; sprinkle with pine nuts.

PER SERVING:
Calories: 449
Protein (g): 14.6
Carbohydrate (g): 76.7
Fat (g): 10.4
Saturated Fat (g): 1.5
Cholesterol (mg): 0
Dietary Fiber (g): 7.7
Sodium (mg): 156

BUCATINI WITH BRUSSELS SPROUTS AND WALNUTS

This dish provides an interesting contrast of textures and hot and cold ingredients.

PREP/COOK TIME:
20–25 minutes
SERVINGS: *4*

12	ounces Brussels sprouts, cut into halves
2	teaspoons minced garlic
1–2	tablespoons olive oil
8	ounces bucatini, *or* spaghetti, cooked, warm
2	cups seeded, chopped Italian plum tomatoes
⅔	cup minced parsley
¼	cup plain bread crumbs, toasted
½	cup chopped walnuts
2–4	tablespoons shredded Parmesan cheese
	Salt and pepper, to taste

Cook Brussels sprouts in 2 inches simmering water until crisp-tender, about 8 minutes; drain.

Saute garlic in oil in medium skillet 1 to 2 minutes; add Brussels sprouts and cook 2 to 3 minutes longer.

Toss pasta with sprouts mixture, tomatoes, parsley, bread crumbs, walnuts, and Parmesan cheese in serving bowl; season to taste with salt and pepper.

PER SERVING:
Calories: 438
Protein (g): 17
Carbohydrate (g): 62.8
Fat (g): 15
Saturated Fat (g): 1.8
Cholesterol (mg): 2
Dietary Fiber (g): 8.1
Sodium (mg): 144

91

MAFALDE WITH SWEET POTATOES AND KALE

L

PREPARATION TIME:
10–15 minutes
COOKING TIME:
15–20 minutes
SERVINGS: 4

Mafalde is a flat pasta with ruffled edges that looks like a miniature version of lasagne noodles. Any flat noodle or even spaghetti can be substituted.

2   medium-size sweet potatoes, peeled, cubed (¾ inch)
2   medium onions, each cut into 8 wedges and halved
2   teaspoons minced garlic
2   tablespoons olive oil
4   cups sliced kale, *or* Swiss chard
½   cup water
8   ounces mafalde, cooked, warm
2   tablespoons shredded Parmesan cheese

Simmer sweet potatoes in water to cover in medium saucepan until barely tender, 5 to 8 minutes. Drain.

Saute onions and garlic in oil in large skillet 2 to 3 minutes. Add potatoes, kale, and ½ cup water; heat to boiling. Reduce heat and simmer, covered, until kale and potatoes are tender and water absorbed, 10 to 12 minutes.

Toss vegetable mixture and pasta in serving bowl; sprinkle with cheese.

PER SERVING:
Calories: 405
Protein (g): 12.4
Carbohydrate (g): 69
Fat (g): 9.2
Saturated Fat (g): 1.6
Cholesterol (mg): 2
Dietary Fiber (g): 7.4
Sodium (mg): 86

TAGLIATELLE WITH CHILI-MUSHROOM STROGANOFF SAUCE

L

Shiitake mushrooms and dried ancho chilies add unique flavors to this aromatic pasta sauce. The chilies can be quite hot, so adjust the amount according to your taste.

PREPARATION TIME:

30–35 minutes

COOKING TIME:

10–15 minutes

SERVINGS: *6*

1	package (1¾ ounces) dried shiitake mushrooms
1–2	dried ancho chilies
3	cups boiling water, divided
2	cups vegetable broth, divided
1	cup chopped onion
8	ounces white mushrooms, halved or quartered
2	tablespoons margarine
¼	cup all-purpose flour
½	teaspoon dried thyme leaves
1	cup reduced-fat sour cream
1	teaspoon Dijon-style mustard
	Salt and pepper, to taste
12	ounces tagliatelle (flat pasta), *or* fettuccine, cooked, warm
	Minced parsley, for garnish

Place shiitake mushrooms and chilies in separate bowls; pour 2 cups boiling water over the mushrooms and 1 cup over the chilies. Let stand until vegetables are softened, about 10 minutes.

Drain mushrooms, reserving liquid. Remove tough centers from mushrooms and slice. Drain chilies, discarding liquid. Process chilies and 1 cup broth in blender or food processor until smooth.

Saute onion, shiitake and white mushrooms in margarine in large skillet until wilted, about 5 minutes. Stir in flour; cook 1 minute longer, stirring frequently. Stir in reserved mushroom liquid, chili mixture, remaining 1 cup broth, and thyme. Heat to boiling; reduce heat and simmer, covered, until shiitake mushrooms are tender, 10 to 15 minutes. Simmer uncovered, if necessary, until thickened.

93

Stir in sour cream and mustard; cook until hot through, 2 to 3 minutes. Season to taste with salt and pepper. Toss pasta with sauce in serving bowl; sprinkle generously with parsley.

PER SERVING:
Calories: 371
Protein (g): 13.1
Carbohydrate (g): 60.8
Fat (g): 8.9
Saturated Fat (g): 3.6
Cholesterol (mg): 13.4
Dietary Fiber (g): 4.1
Sodium (mg): 418

CURRIED TORTELLINI WITH GREEN BEANS AND SQUASH

Coconut milk adds a subtle Asian accent to this colorful pasta combination.

1 1/3 cups chopped onions

2/3 cup chopped red, *or* green, bell pepper

2 teaspoons minced garlic

1 tablespoon vegetable oil

1 teaspoon curry powder

2 cups halved Italian, *or* regular, green beans

2 cups cubed (1/2 inch) peeled, seeded butternut, *or* acorn, squash

1/4 cup water

1 cup reduced-fat coconut milk

2 packages (9 ounces each) fresh mushroom, *or* herb, tortellini, cooked, warm

Salt and pepper, to taste

3 tablespoons finely chopped cilantro

Saute onions, bell pepper, and garlic in oil in large skillet 4 minutes. Stir in curry powder; cook 1 to 2 minutes longer.

Add green beans, squash, and water to skillet; heat to boiling. Reduce heat and simmer, covered, until vegetables are tender and water gone, 10 to 12 minutes. Stir in coconut milk and cook over medium heat until hot, 2 to 3 minutes. Stir in tortellini. Season to taste with salt and pepper.

Spoon pasta mixture into serving bowl; sprinkle with cilantro.

PREP/COOK TIME:
25–30 minutes
SERVINGS: **6**

PER SERVING:
Calories: 275
Protein (g): 10.7
Carbohydrate (g): 42
Fat (g): 8.5
Saturated Fat (g): 2
Cholesterol (mg): 13.3
Dietary Fiber (g): 7
Sodium (mg): 277

CHINESE NOODLES WITH SWEET POTATOES AND SNOW PEAS

Fresh Chinese noodles and oriental ingredients make this pasta dish special.

PREP/COOK TIME:

30–35 minutes

SERVINGS: 4

	Oriental-flavored vegetable cooking spray
2	cups cubed (½ inch), peeled, sweet potatoes
¾	cup diagonally sliced green onions and tops
3	teaspoons minced garlic
1–2	teaspoons minced gingerroot
2	cups halved snow peas
½	cup chopped red, *or* green, bell pepper
¾	cup vegetable broth
1–2	teaspoons tamari soy sauce
1½	teaspoons cornstarch
	Salt and pepper, to taste
1–2	teaspoons toasted sesame seeds
1	package (8 ounces) fresh Chinese egg noodles, cooked, warm

Spray wok or large skillet with cooking spray; heat over medium heat until hot. Stir-fry potatoes, green onions, garlic, and gingerroot 2 to 3 minutes; cook, covered, over low heat until potatoes are almost tender, 10 to 12 minutes, stirring occasionally.

Add snow peas and bell pepper to wok; stir-fry over medium heat until peas are crisp-tender, about 5 minutes. Combine broth, soy sauce, and cornstarch; add to wok and heat to boiling. Boil, stirring constantly, until thickened, about 1 minute. Season to taste with salt and pepper.

Spoon vegetable mixture over noodles in serving bowl; sprinkle with sesame seeds.

PER SERVING:
Calories: 298
Protein (g): 10.5
Carbohydrate (g): 62
Fat (g): 5.8
Saturated Fat (g): 0.5
Cholesterol (mg): 4.4
Dietary Fiber (g): 5.3
Sodium (mg): 988

PASTA WITH GOAT'S CHEESE AND ONION CONFIT

Try this dish with flavored specialty pastas such as dried mushroom, herb, or black pepper.

L

PREPARATION TIME:

10–15 minutes

COOKING TIME:

30–35 minutes

SERVINGS: *4*

	Olive oil cooking spray
4	cups thinly sliced onions
1	teaspoon minced garlic
½	teaspoon dried sage leaves
½	teaspoon dried rosemary leaves
1	teaspoon sugar
½	cup dry white wine, *or* non-fat milk
2	ounces fat-free cream cheese
2–3	ounces goat's cheese
	Salt and white pepper, to taste
8	ounces whole wheat, *or* plain, thin spaghetti, cooked, warm
4	tablespoons coarsely chopped walnuts

Spray large skillet with cooking spray; heat over medium heat until hot. Add onions; cook, covered, over medium-low to low heat until onions are very soft, about 20 minutes.

Stir garlic, sage, rosemary, and sugar into onions; cook, uncovered, over medium-low to low heat until onions are caramelized and brown, 10 to 15 minutes. Stir in wine; simmer 2 to 3 minutes longer. Stir in cream cheese and goat's cheese; cook over low heat, stirring, until melted, 2 to 3 minutes. Season to taste with salt and white pepper.

Toss pasta and onion mixture on serving platter; sprinkle with walnuts.

PER SERVING:
Calories: 373
Protein (g): 16.4
Carbohydrate (g): 54.8
Fat (g): 9.9
Saturated Fat (g): 3.5
Cholesterol (mg): 12.3
Dietary Fiber (g): 9.7
Sodium (mg): 161

STIR-FRIED RICE NOODLES WITH VEGETABLES

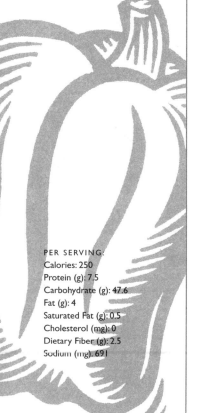

V

PREP/COOK TIME:

30–35 minutes

SERVINGS: *4*

(about 1 1/2 cups each)

PER SERVING:
Calories: 250
Protein (g): 7.5
Carbohydrate (g): 47.6
Fat (g): 4
Saturated Fat (g): 0.5
Cholesterol (mg): 0
Dietary Fiber (g): 2.5
Sodium (mg): 691

Rice noodles are also called cellophane noodles, or "bihon." The dried noodles are soaked in cold water to soften, then drained before using.

1	package (8 ounces) rice noodles
	Cold water
1	tablespoon vegetable oil
1	cup halved green beans
1	cup cubed yellow summer squash
1/2	cup sliced red, *or* green, bell pepper
4	green onions and tops, thinly sliced
1	tablespoon finely chopped fresh gingerroot
2	cups thinly sliced napa cabbage
1	cup vegetable broth
2–3	teaspoons soy sauce
1/2–1	teaspoon Szechwan chili sauce

Place noodles in large bowl; pour cold water over to cover. While you prepare vegetables, let noodles stand until separate and soft, about 15 minutes; drain.

Heat oil in wok or skillet over medium-high heat until hot. Add green beans, squash, bell pepper, green onions, and gingerroot. Stir-fry until vegetables are tender, 8 to 10 minutes.

Add cabbage to wok; stir-fry just until cabbage turns bright in color, about 1 minute. Stir in drained noodles, broth, soy sauce, and chili sauce. Heat to boiling; reduce heat and simmer, uncovered, until noodles have absorbed all liquid, about 5 minutes.

great grains

Falafel Dinner Loaf

Eggplant Polenta Stack

Two-Cheese Risotto

Mexican-Style Vegetables and Rice

Quinoa with Roasted Eggplant and Squash

Asian Fried Rice

Mushroom and Asparagus Pilaf

Curried Couscous and Vegetables

Sweet Bulgur Pilaf

Vegetable Salad with Millet

Kasha with Green Veggies

FALAFEL DINNER LOAF

*Dried fruit provides a marvelous sweet accent in this easy-to-make loaf.
We think it's also terrific served cold for warm-weather dining.*

LO

1 package (6 ounces) falafel mix
½ cup shredded zucchini
½ cup dried fruit bits, *or* chopped mixed dried fruit
¼ cup coarsely chopped toasted pecans
2 tablespoons thinly sliced green onions and tops
2 eggs, *or* ½ cup no-cholesterol egg product
¾ cup reduced-fat plain yogurt

PREPARATION TIME:
15 minutes
BAKING TIME:
30 minutes
SERVINGS: **4**

Prepare falafel mix with water according to package directions; mix in remaining ingredients, except yogurt. Pack mixture into lightly greased 7 ½ x 3 ½-inch loaf pan.

Bake at 350 degrees until mixture is set, about 30 minutes. Invert loaf onto serving plate; slice and serve with dollops of yogurt.

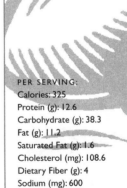

PER SERVING:
Calories: 325
Protein (g): 12.6
Carbohydrate (g): 38.3
Fat (g): 11.2
Saturated Fat (g): 1.6
Cholesterol (mg): 108.6
Dietary Fiber (g): 4
Sodium (mg): 600

EGGPLANT POLENTA STACK

LO

PREPARATION TIME:
10–15 minutes

COOKING/BAKING TIME:
30 minutes

SERVINGS: *4*

Purchase packaged flavored polenta in the produce section; choose any favorite for this dish.

8	slices (¾ inch) eggplant (about 1 pound)
2	egg whites, lightly beaten, *or* ¼ cup no-cholesterol egg product
½	cup Italian-seasoned dry bread crumbs
¼	cup grated Parmesan cheese
	Olive oil cooking spray
1	package (16 ounces) prepared Italian-herb polenta, cut into 8 slices
8	slices (½ inch) tomato
	Salt and pepper, to taste
2–4	ounces reduced-fat feta, *or* goat's cheese, crumbled

Dip eggplant slices in egg whites and coat with combined bread crumbs and Parmesan cheese. Spray large skillet with cooking spray and heat over medium heat until hot. Cook eggplant until browned on the bottom, about 10 minutes; spray tops of slices with cooking spray and turn. Cook until eggplant is tender and browned on other side, about 10 minutes longer.

Arrange eggplant in baking pan; top each with a slice of polenta and tomato. Sprinkle tomatoes with salt and pepper; sprinkle with feta cheese.

Bake at 450 degrees until tomatoes are hot and cheese lightly browned, about 10 minutes.

PER SERVING:
Calories: 222
Protein (g): 10.9
Carbohydrate (g): 35
Fat (g): 4.5
Saturated Fat (g): 2.4
Cholesterol (mg): 9
Dietary Fiber (g): 5.7
Sodium (mg): 624

TWO-CHEESE RISOTTO

A flavorful risotto quickly prepared with a simplified method that requires little stirring. Serve with a salad and steamed green vegetable for a simple but elegant meal.

PREPARATION TIME:

10 minutes

COOKING TIME:

30–35 minutes

SERVINGS: *4*

(about 1 cup each)

Vegetable cooking spray
½ cup finely chopped onion
1 cup arborio rice
2½ cups reduced-sodium vegetable broth
½ cup dry white wine
1 cup (4 ounces) shredded Parmesan cheese
¼–½ cup (1–2 ounces) crumbled blue cheese
2–3 tablespoons chopped chives, *or* Italian parsley
Salt and pepper, to taste

Spray large saucepan with cooking spray; heat over medium heat until hot. Add onion and saute until tender, 3 to 4 minutes. Add rice to saucepan; cook over medium heat until beginning to brown, 3 to 4 minutes.

Add vegetable broth and wine to saucepan; heat to boiling. Reduce heat and simmer, covered, until rice is tender and liquid absorbed, 25 to 30 minutes, stirring occasionally. Remove from heat; stir in cheeses and chives. Season to taste with salt and pepper.

PER SERVING:
Calories: 345
Protein (g): 13.9
Carbohydrate (g): 47.3
Fat (g): 8.3
Saturated Fat (g): 5.2
Cholesterol (mg): 21.1
Dietary Fiber (g): 1.8
Sodium (mg): 525

MEXICAN-STYLE VEGETABLES AND RICE

L

PREPARATION TIME:
15 minutes

COOKING TIME:
15–20 minutes

SERVINGS: *6*
(about 1¼ cups each)

PER SERVING:
Calories: 270
Protein (g): 11.2
Carbohydrate (g): 41.7
Fat (g): 6.8
Saturated Fat (g): 3.2
Cholesterol (mg): 15.1
Dietary Fiber (g): 3.3
Sodium (mg): 140

These cheesy vegetables make a delicious filling for soft tacos.

1½	cups frozen pepper stir-fry blend
1½	teaspoons minced garlic
1	jalapeño chili, finely chopped
1	tablespoon vegetable oil
2	medium chayote squash, peeled, seeded, cubed
2	cups halved small cremini mushrooms
1	cup frozen, *or* canned, drained, whole-kernel corn
¾	teaspoon dried oregano leaves
½	teaspoon ground cumin
½	teaspoon chili powder
4	cups cooked white, *or* brown, rice
	Salt and pepper, to taste
¾	cup (3 ounces) shredded reduced-fat Monterey Jack cheese
6	tablespoons reduced-fat sour cream
2	green onions and tops, sliced

Saute pepper blend, garlic, and jalapeño chili in oil in large skillet over medium heat 5 minutes; add squash, mushrooms, corn, oregano, cumin, and chili powder. Cook, covered, over medium heat until squash and mushrooms are tender, 8 to 10 minutes, stirring occasionally. Stir in rice; season to taste with salt and pepper.

Sprinkle cheese over vegetable mixture; cook, covered, until cheese melts, 3 to 5 minutes. Garnish with sour cream and green onions.

QUINOA WITH ROASTED EGGPLANT AND SQUASH

Grain recipes are versatile, as almost any grain can be used in them. Couscous, millet, or kasha would be excellent alternates in this recipe.

Garlic-flavored vegetable cooking spray
1 small butternut squash, peeled, seeded, cubed
1 medium eggplant, unpeeled, cubed
2 medium onions, cut into wedges
2 large red, *or* green, bell peppers, cored, cut into thick slices
1 teaspoon dried rosemary leaves
½ teaspoon dried savory leaves
½ teaspoon dried thyme leaves
2 cups vegetable broth
1 cup quinoa
Salt and pepper, to taste

Spray aluminum foil-lined jelly roll pan with cooking spray; arrange vegetables in single layer on pan. Spray vegetables generously with cooking spray; sprinkle with herbs. Roast at 450 degrees until vegetables are tender, about 30 minutes.

While vegetables are roasting, heat broth to boiling in medium saucepan; add quinoa. Reduce heat and simmer, covered, until quinoa is tender and stock absorbed, about 15 minutes. Combine quinoa and warm vegetables in serving bowl; season to taste with salt and pepper.

PREP/COOK TIME:
15 minutes
BAKING TIME:
30 minutes
SERVINGS: *4*
(about 1½ cups each)

PER SERVING:
Calories: 275
Protein (g): 9.4
Carbohydrate (g): 56.6
Fat (g): 3.5
Saturated Fat (g): 0.4
Cholesterol (mg): 0
Dietary Fiber (g): 10.6
Sodium (mg): 519

ASIAN FRIED RICE

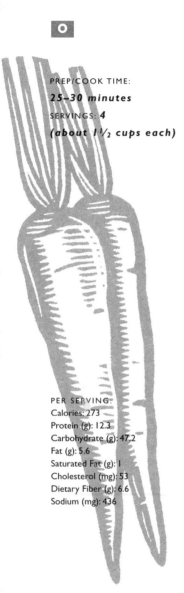

PREP/COOK TIME:
25–30 minutes
SERVINGS: **4**
(about 1 1/2 cups each)

The combination of wild and white rice adds a new dimension to an Asian favorite. Lightly scrambled egg is a traditional addition to many fried rice recipes; it can be omitted, if desired.

1 package (6 1/4 ounces) quick-cooking long-grain and wild rice
2 cups broccoli florets
2 ounces snow peas, cut into halves
2 medium carrots, sliced
3/4 cup bean sprouts
3/4 cup sliced shiitake, *or* white, mushrooms
1/2 cup chopped red, *or* green, bell pepper
1 teaspoon minced garlic
1 teaspoon finely chopped gingerroot
1–2 tablespoons vegetable oil
1/2 cup vegetable broth
2 tablespoons reduced-sodium soy sauce
1 egg, lightly scrambled, crumbled

Cook rice according to package directions, discarding seasoning packet.

Stir-fry vegetables, garlic, and gingerroot in oil in wok over medium-high heat until crisp-tender, 5 to 8 minutes.

Add broth and soy sauce to wok; stir in rice and scrambled egg and cook 2 to 3 minutes more.

PER SERVING:
Calories: 273
Protein (g): 12.3
Carbohydrate (g): 47.2
Fat (g): 5.6
Saturated Fat (g): 1
Cholesterol (mg): 53
Dietary Fiber (g): 6.6
Sodium (mg): 436

MUSHROOM AND ASPARAGUS PILAF

The dried Chinese black or shiitake mushrooms impart a hearty, woodsy flavor to the pilaf. The mushrooms are available in large supermarkets or oriental groceries.

3 ⅓   cups vegetable broth, divided
2   cups dried Chinese mushrooms
    Vegetable cooking spray
1 ½   cups chopped onions
2   teaspoons minced garlic
2   teaspoons bouquet garni
1 ½   pounds asparagus, cut into 1½-inch pieces
¼   cup dry sherry, *or* water
2   packages (6 ounces each) tabouleh wheat salad mix
¼   teaspoon red pepper sauce
    Salt and pepper, to taste
4   green onions and tops, thinly sliced
¼   cup toasted pecan halves

Heat 2 cups broth to boiling; pour over mushrooms in bowl and let stand until mushrooms are softened, about 10 minutes. Drain, reserving broth. Slice mushrooms, discarding tough stems.

Spray large skillet with cooking spray; heat over medium heat until hot. Saute mushrooms, onions, garlic, and herbs until onions are tender, about 5 minutes. Add asparagus; saute 5 minutes more.

Add sherry, reserved broth from mushrooms, and remaining 1⅓ cups broth to skillet; heat to boiling. Stir in wheat pilaf (discard spice packet). Reduce heat and simmer, covered, until broth is absorbed and pilaf is tender, 3 to 5 minutes. Stir in red pepper sauce; season to taste with salt and pepper. Spoon into serving bowl; sprinkle with green onions and pecans.

V

PREP/COOK TIME:
25–30 minutes
SERVINGS: *8*
(about 1 ¼ cups each)

PER SERVING:
Calories: 241
Protein (g): 8.3
Carbohydrate (g): 42.1
Fat (g): 3.7
Saturated Fat (g): 0.3
Cholesterol (mg): 0
Dietary Fiber (g): 3.9
Sodium (mg): 927

CURRIED COUSCOUS AND VEGETABLES

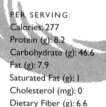

L

PREPARATION TIME:
15–20 minutes
COOKING TIME:
20–25 minutes
SERVINGS: *4*
(about 1 1/2 cups each)

PER SERVING:
Calories: 277
Protein (g): 8.2
Carbohydrate (g): 46.6
Fat (g): 7.9
Saturated Fat (g): 1
Cholesterol (mg): 0
Dietary Fiber (g): 6.6
Sodium (mg): 276

Couscous, a staple in Mediterranean countries, is one of the fastest, easiest grains to cook. Serve this dish with a selection of condiments so that the dish can be enjoyed with a variety of flavor accents.

8	ounces fresh, *or* frozen, thawed, whole okra
1	cup chopped onion
1	teaspoon minced garlic
2	tablespoons vegetable oil
1	cup frozen, *or* canned, drained, whole-kernel corn
1	cup sliced mushrooms
2	medium carrots, sliced
1 1/2	teaspoons curry powder
1	cup vegetable broth
2/3	cup couscous
1	medium tomato, chopped
	Salt and pepper, to taste

Condiments: plain reduced-fat yogurt, chopped cucumber, chopped peanuts, raisins (not included in nutritional data)

Saute okra, onion, and garlic in oil in large saucepan 5 minutes. Stir in corn, mushrooms, carrots, and curry powder; cook 2 minutes more.

Add broth to saucepan and heat to boiling; reduce heat and simmer, covered, until vegetables are tender, 8 to 10 minutes. Stir in couscous (discard spice packet) and tomato. Remove from heat and let stand, covered, until couscous is tender and broth absorbed, about 5 minutes. Season to taste with salt and pepper.

Spoon couscous mixture into serving bowl; serve with condiments.

SWEET BULGUR PILAF

A pilaf with sweet accents of squash, raisins, and cinnamon.

- ⅔ cup thinly sliced green onions and tops
- 1 teaspoon minced garlic
- 1 cup bulgur
- 1–2 tablespoons olive oil
- 2¼ cups vegetable broth
- ½–¾ teaspoon ground cinnamon
- 2 cups cubed, peeled, seeded butternut, *or* acorn, squash
- ¼ cup currants, *or* raisins
- ¼ cup pine nuts, toasted
- ¼ cup finely chopped parsley
- Salt and pepper, to taste

Saute green onions, garlic, and bulgur in oil in large saucepan over medium heat until onions are tender, about 3 minutes. Stir in broth and cinnamon and heat to boiling; reduce heat and simmer, covered, 10 minutes.

Stir squash and currants into bulgur mixture; simmer, covered, until squash is tender, about 15 minutes. Stir in pine nuts and parsley; season to taste with salt and pepper.

PREPARATION TIME:
10–15 minutes
COOKING TIME:
30 minutes
SERVINGS: **4**
(about 1 cup each)

PER SERVING:
Calories: 267
Protein (g): 9.1
Carbohydrate (g): 42.3
Fat (g): 9.6
Saturated Fat (g): 1.3
Cholesterol (mg): 0
Dietary Fiber (g): 11
Sodium (mg): 576

VEGETABLE SALAD WITH MILLET

PREPARATION TIME:
20–25 minutes

COOKING TIME:
15–20 minutes

SERVINGS: *6*

(about 1 1/3 cups each)

Finely chop the vegetables by hand or in a food processor. Serve the salad in bowls, in hollowed out beefsteak tomato halves, or use it as a filling for warm pita breads.

1 1/4	cups millet
3 1/3	cups water
1/2	cup sliced celery
1/2	medium red, *or* green, bell pepper, sliced
4	green onions and tops, sliced
1	medium carrot, sliced
4	tablespoons finely chopped fresh basil, *or* 2 teaspoons dried basil leaves
1/2	head iceberg lettuce, sliced
1	medium tomato, coarsely chopped
	Oregano Vinaigrette (recipe follows)
	Salt and pepper, to taste
	Spinach, *or* lettuce leaves, for garnish
4	pita breads

Cook millet in large saucepan over medium heat until toasted, 2 to 3 minutes. Add water and heat to boiling; reduce heat and simmer, covered, until millet is tender and liquid absorbed, about 15 to 20 minutes. Spread millet on large plate and refrigerate until cool, 10 to 15 minutes.

Combine celery, bell pepper, green onions, carrot, and basil in food processor; process, using pulse technique, until finely chopped. Add mixture to large bowl.

Add lettuce to food processor; process, using pulse technique, until finely chopped. Add mixture to bowl with vegetables.

Add tomato and millet to vegetable mixture and toss; drizzle with Oregano Vinaigrette and toss. Season to taste with salt and pepper. Spoon salad into spinach-lined salad bowls; serve with pita breads.

OREGANO VINAIGRETTE

makes about ⅓ cup

   3 – 4 tablespoons olive oil
     3 tablespoons white wine vinegar
     I teaspoon dried oregano leaves

Mix all ingredients; refrigerate until ready to serve.

PER SERVING:
Calories: 357
Protein (g): 9.9
Carbohydrate (g): 59.5
Fat (g): 9.8
Saturated Fat (g): 1.4
Cholesterol (mg): 0
Dietary Fiber (g): 8.6
Sodium (mg): 250

KASHA WITH GREEN VEGGIES

PREPARATION TIME:

15 minutes

COOKING TIME:

25–30 minutes

SERVINGS: **6**

Kasha is buckwheat groats that have been roasted. Traditionally, kasha is mixed with raw egg and cooked in a skillet until dry, which keeps the grains separate while cooking.

1½ cups kasha
1 egg, beaten
1 large green bell pepper, chopped
½ cup sliced green onions and tops
1 teaspoon minced garlic
1 tablespoon olive oil
4 cups vegetable broth
½ teaspoon dried marjoram leaves
¼ teaspoon dried thyme leaves
12 ounces broccoli rabe, cut into 1-inch pieces
Salt and pepper, to taste

Mix kasha and egg in bowl; transfer to large skillet and cook over medium heat until kasha is dry and grains are separated, 3 to 4 minutes.

Saute bell pepper, green onions, and garlic in oil in large saucepan until tender, about 5 minutes. Add kasha, broth, and herbs to saucepan; heat to boiling. Reduce heat and simmer, covered, until kasha is tender and liquid absorbed, 25 to 30 minutes.

While kasha is cooking, cook broccoli rabe in 1-inch simmering water until crisp-tender, about 8 minutes; drain. Stir into kasha mixture; season to taste with salt and pepper.

PER SERVING:
Calories: 208
Protein (g): 9.1
Carbohydrate (g): 37
Fat (g): 5.1
Saturated Fat (g): 0.8
Cholesterol (mg): 35.3
Dietary Fiber (g): 6.3
Sodium (mg): 698

bountiful beans

Black Bean Soup with Sun-Dried Tomatoes and Cilantro Cream

Bean and Barley Soup

Garlicky Lima Bean Soup

Curried Bean Soup

Yellow Squash and White Bean Chili

Pintos, Greens, and Rice

Bourbon Street Red Beans and Rice

Santa Fe Baked Beans

Tuscan Bean Bake

Stir-Fried Beans and Greens

Bean, Tomato, and Bread Salad

Lentil Salad with Feta Cheese

BLACK BEAN SOUP WITH SUN-DRIED TOMATOES AND CILANTRO CREAM

L

Although this soup may be served with plain sour cream, the Cilantro Cream adds a fresh accent to a Southwestern favorite.

PREPARATION TIME:

15 minutes

COOKING TIME:

15 minutes

SERVINGS: **4**

(about 1 ½ cup each)

1	cup chopped onion
1	teaspoon minced garlic
1	jalapeño chili, minced
1–2	tablespoons vegetable oil
3	cups vegetable broth
2	cans (15 ounces each) black beans, rinsed, drained
¾	cup sun-dried tomatoes (not in oil)
¾	teaspoon ground cumin
½	teaspoon dried oregano leaves
¼–½	teaspoon hot pepper sauce
	Salt and pepper, to taste
¼	cup finely chopped cilantro
	Cilantro Cream (recipe follows), *or* ½ cup fat-free sour cream

Saute onion, garlic, and jalapeño chili in oil in large saucepan 5 minutes. Add broth, beans, sun-dried tomatoes, cumin, and oregano to saucepan; heat to boiling. Reduce heat and simmer, covered, 10 minutes. Season to taste with hot pepper sauce, salt, and pepper; stir in cilantro.

Process soup mixture in food processor or blender until smooth. Pour into bowls; garnish with dollops of Cilantro Cream.

CILANTRO CREAM

makes about 1/2 cup

- 1/2 cup fat-free sour cream
- 2 tablespoons minced cilantro
- 1 teaspoon lemon, *or* lime, juice
- 3/4 teaspoon ground coriander
- 2–3 dashes white pepper

Mix all ingredients.

PER SERVING:
Calories: 292
Protein (g): 17.3
Carbohydrate (g): 46.3
Fat (g): 6.4
Saturated Fat (g): 0.5
Cholesterol (mg): 0
Dietary Fiber (g): 13.8
Sodium (mg): 1646

BEAN AND BARLEY SOUP

A soup that can be easily increased to serve a crowd; make it a day ahead of time for best flavor.

V

PREPARATION TIME:

15 minutes

COOKING TIME:

25–30 minutes

SERVINGS: *8*

(about 1 1/2 cups each)

1	cup chopped onion
3/4	cup chopped red, *or* green, bell pepper
2	teaspoons minced roasted garlic
2	tablespoons olive oil
1	tablespoon flour
1 1/2	teaspoons dried Italian seasoning
7	cups vegetable broth
2	cans (15 ounces each) cannellini, *or* Great Northern, beans, rinsed, drained
2	tablespoons tomato paste
1/2	cup quick-cooking barley
1	large Idaho potato, unpeeled, cut into 1/2-inch pieces
1	cup sliced carrots
1	cup packed baby spinach leaves
	Salt and pepper, to taste

Saute onion, bell pepper, and garlic in oil in Dutch oven 5 minutes. Add flour and Italian seasoning; cook 1 to 2 minutes longer.

Add remaining ingredients, except spinach, salt, and pepper, to Dutch oven; heat to boiling. Reduce heat and simmer, uncovered, 20 to 25 minutes, adding spinach during last 5 minutes of cooking time. Season to taste with salt and pepper.

PER SERVING:
Calories: 211
Protein (g): 8.5
Carbohydrate (g): 35.1
Fat (g): 5.1
Saturated Fat (g): 0.5
Cholesterol (mg): 0
Dietary Fiber (g): 7.7
Sodium (mg): 1142

GARLICKY LIMA BEAN SOUP

PREPARATION TIME:

15 minutes

COOKING TIME:

25 minutes

SERVINGS: *4*

(about 1½ cups each)

PER SERVING:
Calories: 294
Protein (g): 15.9
Carbohydrate (g): 49.5
Fat (g): 5.4
Saturated Fat (g): 0.9
Cholesterol (mg): 2.3
Dietary Fiber (g): 13.4
Sodium (mg): 1579

For those who love garlic! The amount of garlic can be reduced if you prefer a more subtle dish. You'll find jarred, peeled garlic in the produce section of many supermarkets.

2	cups chopped onions
10	large cloves garlic, peeled, quartered
1	teaspoon crushed red pepper
1	tablespoon vegetable oil
2	cans (17 ounces each) lima beans, rinsed, drained
3	cups vegetable broth
1	teaspoon dried thyme leaves
½	cup 2% reduced-fat milk
	Salt and white pepper, to taste
	Parsley, finely chopped, for garnish

Cook onions, garlic, and red pepper in oil in large saucepan, covered, over medium heat 10 minutes. Add beans, broth, and thyme to saucepan; heat to boiling. Reduce heat and simmer, covered, 10 minutes.

Process soup in food processor or blender until smooth; return to saucepan. Stir in milk; heat over medium heat until hot, 2 to 3 minutes. Season to taste with salt and white pepper.

Serve soup in bowls; sprinkle with parsley.

CURRIED BEAN SOUP

Use any white bean, such as cannellini, navy, soy, lima, or garbanzo, in this rich, aromatic soup.

L

1 cup chopped onion
1 cup sliced leek (white part only)
3 teaspoons minced garlic
1 tablespoon curry powder
2 tablespoons margarine
2 cans (15 ounces each) Great Northern beans, rinsed, drained
3 1/2 cups vegetable broth
1/2 cup 2% reduced-fat milk
Salt and pepper, to taste
6 tablespoons reduced-fat sour cream, *or* plain yogurt
3 tablespoons finely chopped cilantro
2 tablespoons finely chopped red, *or* green, bell pepper

PREPARATION TIME:

10 minutes

COOKING TIME:

15 minutes

SERVINGS: *4*

(about 1 1/2 cups each)

Saute onion, leek, garlic, and curry powder in margarine in large saucepan 5 minutes. Add beans and broth to saucepan; heat to boiling. Reduce heat and simmer, covered, 5 minutes.

Process bean mixture in food processor or blender until smooth; return to saucepan. Stir in milk; cook over medium heat until hot, 2 to 3 minutes. Season to taste with salt and pepper.

Serve soup in bowls; top each with dollops of sour cream. Sprinkle with cilantro and bell pepper.

PER SERVING:
Calories: 278
Protein (g): 16.1
Carbohydrate (g): 44.7
Fat (g): 9.4
Saturated Fat (g): 3
Cholesterol (mg): 9.8
Dietary Fiber (g): 12.2
Sodium (mg): 1828

YELLOW SQUASH AND WHITE BEAN CHILI

PREPARATION TIME:

15 minutes

COOKING TIME:

25–30 minutes

SERVINGS: 4

(about 1 1/2 cups each)

PER SERVING:
Calories: 218
Protein (g): 13.3
Carbohydrate (g): 42.7
Fat (g): 4.6
Saturated Fat (g): 0.6
Cholesterol (mg): 0
Dietary Fiber (g): 13.2
Sodium (mg): 1344

Add a minced jalapeño if you like your chili hot!

2 cups chopped onions
1 cup chopped yellow bell pepper
2 teaspoons minced garlic
2 teaspoons cumin seeds
1–2 tablespoons olive oil
1 medium-size yellow summer squash, cubed
2 cans (15 ounces each) Great Northern beans, rinsed, drained
2 cups vegetable broth
1/2 cup dry white wine, optional
1 teaspoon dried oregano leaves
1/2 teaspoon ground cinnamon
2 teaspoons chili powder
  Salt and pepper, to taste
  Finely chopped tomato and cilantro, for garnish

Saute onions, bell pepper, garlic, and cumin seeds in oil in large saucepan 5 minutes. Add remaining ingredients, except salt and pepper and garnishes, to saucepan; heat to boiling. Reduce heat and simmer, covered, until vegetables are tender, about 15 minutes. Simmer, uncovered, until thickened, 5 to 10 minutes. Season to taste with salt and pepper.

Serve soup in bowls; sprinkle with tomato and cilantro.

PINTOS, GREENS, AND RICE

The chilies and cayenne pepper in this heartily spiced dish can be decreased if less hotness is desired.

PREPARATION TIME:

15 minutes

COOKING TIME:

25 minutes

SERVINGS: *8*

(about 1¼ cups each)

1	cup chopped onion
1	large poblano chili, chopped
2	teaspoons minced garlic
1	tablespoon finely chopped gingerroot
2	serrano chilies, finely chopped
2	tablespoons olive oil
2–3	teaspoons chili powder
2	teaspoons dried oregano leaves
1	teaspoon ground cumin
½	teaspoon cayenne pepper
4	cans (15 ounces each) pinto beans, rinsed, drained
1	can (15 ounces) diced tomatoes, undrained
2	cups coarsely chopped turnip, *or* mustard, greens
	Salt, to taste
4	cups cooked rice, warm

Saute onion, poblano chili, garlic, gingerroot, and serrano chilies in oil in large saucepan 8 minutes. Stir in chili powder, herbs, and cayenne pepper; cook 1 to 2 minutes longer.

Stir in beans, tomatoes, and turnip greens and heat to boiling. Reduce heat and simmer, covered, 10 minutes; uncover and cook until mixture is desired thickness, about 5 minutes. Season to taste with salt.

Spoon rice into bowls; top with beans and greens mixture.

PER SERVING:
Calories: 349
Protein (g): 14.1
Carbohydrate (g): 62
Fat (g): 5.7
Saturated Fat (g): 0.9
Cholesterol (mg): 0
Dietary Fiber (g): 12.6
Sodium (mg): 777

BOURBON STREET RED BEANS AND RICE

PREPARATION TIME:

15 minutes

COOKING TIME:

20–25 minutes

SERVINGS: *4*

(about 1 1/4 cups each)

Our vegetarian version of a New Orleans favorite!

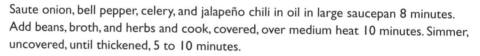

1	cup chopped onion
1	cup chopped green bell pepper
1	cup chopped celery
1/2–1	jalapeño chili, finely chopped
1	tablespoon vegetable oil
2	cans (15 ounces each) red beans, rinsed, drained
3/4	cup vegetable broth
1 1/2	teaspoons dried thyme leaves
1	teaspoon dried oregano leaves
1/2	teaspoon dried sage leaves
1/4–1/2	teaspoon ground cumin
1/4–1/2	teaspoon red pepper sauce
4–6	drops liquid smoke, optional
	Salt, to taste
3	cups cooked rice, warm

PER SERVING:
Calories: 367
Protein (g): 15
Carbohydrate (g): 72.2
Fat (g): 5.1
Saturated Fat (g): 0.6
Cholesterol (mg): 0
Dietary Fiber (g): 11.8
Sodium (mg): 1410

Saute onion, bell pepper, celery, and jalapeño chili in oil in large saucepan 8 minutes. Add beans, broth, and herbs and cook, covered, over medium heat 10 minutes. Simmer, uncovered, until thickened, 5 to 10 minutes.

Stir red pepper sauce and liquid smoke into beans; season to taste with salt. Serve bean mixture over rice in shallow bowls.

SANTA FE BAKED BEANS

These baked beans boast flavors of the great Southwest.

L

PREPARATION TIME:

15 minutes

BAKING TIME:

30 minutes

SERVINGS: *4*

(about 1 1/3 cups each)

- 1 cup chopped onion
- 1/2 cup chopped poblano chili, *or* green bell pepper
- 1/2–1 serrano, *or* jalapeño, chili, finely chopped
- 1 tablespoon olive oil
- 2 cans (15 ounces each) pinto beans, rinsed, drained
- 2 cups frozen, *or* canned, drained, whole-kernel corn
- 6 sun-dried tomatoes (not in oil), cut into fourths
- 2–3 tablespoons honey
- 1/2–1 teaspoon ground cumin
- 1/2 teaspoon dried thyme leaves
- 1/2 cup (2 ounces) crumbled Mexican white, *or* farmer's, cheese
- 1/4 cup finely chopped cilantro

Saute onion and chilies in oil in small skillet until tender, about 5 minutes. Combine all ingredients, except cheese and cilantro, in 1 1/2-quart casserole; sprinkle cheese on top.

Bake, covered, at 350 degrees until bean mixture is hot, about 30 minutes. Sprinkle top of casserole with cilantro before serving.

PER SERVING:
Calories: 442
Protein (g): 18.9
Carbohydrate (g): 76.6
Fat (g): 10
Saturated Fat (g): 3.6
Cholesterol (mg): 13.6
Dietary Fiber (g): 14.1
Sodium (mg): 822

TUSCAN BEAN BAKE

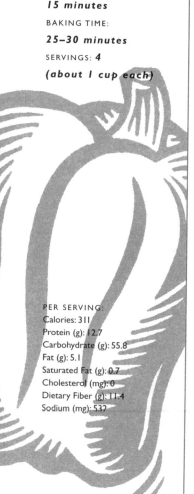

PREPARATION TIME:

15 minutes

BAKING TIME:

25–30 minutes

SERVINGS: **4**

(about 1 cup each)

Easy to combine and bake, the beans are lemon-scented and seasoned with sun-dried tomatoes, garlic, and herbs. Any white beans, such as garbanzo beans, soy beans, or navy beans, can be used.

- 1 cup chopped onion
- 2 teaspoons minced garlic, divided
- ½ cup chopped red, *or* green, bell pepper
- 1 tablespoon olive oil
- 1 large tomato, chopped
- 6 sun-dried tomatoes (not in oil), sliced
- 2–3 teaspoons grated lemon rind
- 1 teaspoon dried sage leaves
- 1 teaspoon dried rosemary leaves
- 2 cans (15 ounces each) cannellini, *or* Great Northern, beans, rinsed, drained
  Salt and pepper, to taste
- 1 cup fresh whole wheat bread crumbs
- ¼ cup minced parsley

PER SERVING:
Calories: 311
Protein (g): 12.7
Carbohydrate (g): 55.8
Fat (g): 5.1
Saturated Fat (g): 0.7
Cholesterol (mg): 0
Dietary Fiber (g): 11.4
Sodium (mg): 532

Saute onion, 1 teaspoon garlic, and bell pepper in oil in large skillet 5 minutes. Add tomato, sun-dried tomatoes, lemon rind, and herbs and saute 2 to 3 minutes longer. Stir in beans and season to taste with salt and pepper; pour into 1½-quart casserole.

Combine bread crumbs, parsley, and remaining 1 teaspoon garlic; sprinkle over top of bean mixture and press lightly onto beans to moisten bread crumbs. Bake, uncovered, at 350 degrees until liquid has evaporated and breadcrumbs are browned, 25 to 30 minutes.

STIR-FRIED BEANS AND GREENS

Oriental foods and flavors combine with black-eyed peas in this sesame-accented main course.

PREP/COOK TIME:

25–30 minutes

SERVINGS: **6**

(about 1 1/4 cups each)

    8 ounces snow peas, diagonally cut into halves
  1/3 cup chopped onion
    1 small red, *or green*, bell pepper, sliced
    1 tablespoon finely chopped gingerroot
    2 teaspoons minced garlic
    1 serrano, *or jalapeño*, chili, finely chopped
    1 tablespoon sesame oil
    3 cups thinly sliced bok choy, *or Chinese cabbage*
    2 cans (15 ounces each) black-eyed peas, rinsed, drained
  1–2 tablespoons reduced-sodium tamari soy sauce
  1–2 teaspoons black bean, *or hoisin*, sauce
    1 package (16 ounces) Chinese-style egg noodles, *or 4 cups cooked rice*
    2 teaspoons toasted sesame seeds

Stir-fry snow peas, onion, bell pepper, gingerroot, garlic, and serrano chili in sesame oil in wok or large skillet 5 to 8 minutes. Stir in bok choy; cook, covered, over medium heat until wilted, 2 to 3 minutes.

Stir black-eyed peas into wok; stir-fry until hot, about 5 minutes. Stir in soy sauce and black bean sauce. Serve mixture over noodles or rice; sprinkle with sesame seeds.

PER SERVING:
Calories: 356
Protein (g): 17.6
Carbohydrate (g): 67.5
Fat (g): 9.6
Saturated Fat (g): 0.9
Cholesterol (mg): 5.9
Dietary Fiber (g): 8.3
Sodium (mg): 1747

BEAN, TOMATO, AND BREAD SALAD

PREPARATION TIME:
15 minutes
BAKING TIME:
10 minutes
SERVINGS: *4*
(about 1 1/2 cups each)

Use summer-ripe tomatoes for best flavor. A favorite purchased salad dressing can be substituted for the homemade.

3	cups cubed (1/2 inch) sourdough bread
	Olive oil cooking spray
2	large tomatoes, cubed
1/2	small red onion, thinly sliced
2	cans (15 ounces each) navy beans, *or* soybeans, rinsed, drained
1	cup chopped roasted red peppers
	Parmesan Vinaigrette (recipe follows), *or* 1 1/2 cups prepared reduced-fat vinaigrette
	Salt and pepper, to taste

Spray bread cubes generously with cooking spray; arrange in single layer on jelly roll pan. Bake at 350 degrees until golden, about 10 minutes, stirring occasionally. Cool.

Combine tomatoes, onion, beans, and roasted red peppers in bowl; pour Parmesan Vinaigrette over and toss. Season to taste with salt and pepper. Add bread cubes to salad and toss; serve immediately.

PARMESAN VINAIGRETTE

makes about 1/2 cup

2–4	tablespoons olive oil
4	tablespoons red wine vinegar
2	tablespoons grated fat-free Parmesan cheese
1/4	cup finely chopped fresh basil leaves, *or* 1 teaspoon dried basil leaves
1	teaspoon minced garlic

Mix all ingredients.

PER SERVING:
Calories: 405
Protein (g): 19.2
Carbohydrate (g): 62.1
Fat (g): 8.7
Saturated Fat (g): 1.5
Cholesterol (mg): 0
Dietary Fiber (g): 12.5
Sodium (mg): 1195

LENTIL SALAD WITH FETA CHEESE

Enjoy the many flavor and texture contrasts in this colorful salad. Cook the lentils just until tender so they retain their shape.

L

PREP/COOK TIME:
35 minutes
SERVINGS: **6**
(about 1 ⅓ cups each)

1½ cups dried brown lentils
  3 cups vegetable broth
  2 medium tomatoes, coarsely chopped
  ½ cup thinly sliced celery
  ½ cup sliced yellow, *or* green, bell pepper
  ½ cup chopped cucumber
  ½ cup chopped onion
½–¾ cup (2–3 ounces) crumbled reduced-fat feta cheese
    Balsamic Dressing (recipe follows), *or* ⅓ cup prepared reduced-fat vinaigrette
    Salt and pepper, to taste
    Lettuce leaves, optional

Wash and sort lentils, discarding any stones. Heat lentils and broth to boiling in large saucepan; reduce heat and simmer, covered, until lentils are just tender, about 25 minutes. Rinse lentils in colander under cold water until cooled to room temperature; drain well.

Combine lentils, vegetables, and cheese in salad bowl; drizzle Balsamic Dressing over and toss. Season to taste with salt and pepper. Serve on lettuce-lined plates.

BALSAMIC DRESSING

makes about ⅓ cup

3–4 tablespoons balsamic, *or* red wine, vinegar
1–2 tablespoons olive oil
  1 teaspoon minced garlic
  ½ teaspoon dried thyme leaves

Mix all ingredients.

PER SERVING:
Calories: 225
Protein (g): 14.7
Carbohydrate (g): 33.7
Fat (g): 4.8
Saturated Fat (g): 1.2
Cholesterol (mg): 3.4
Dietary Fiber (g): 10.9
Sodium (mg): 642

en

easy

tertaining

Black Bean Cheesecake with Salsa

Sweet Potato Chipotle Chili

Curried Couscous with Smoked Tofu

Potato Gnocchi with Sage Cream

Cheese and Vegetable Risotto Pancakes

Fettuccine Florentine Timbale

Artichoke Tortellini Bake

Vietnamese Curried Vegetable and Coconut Stew

Roasted Vegetables, Moo Shu Style

Szechuan Vegetable Stir-Fry

Tempeh Steak with Red and Green Stir-Fry

Ginger Coconut Rice and Sweet Potatoes

Vegetable Strudel with Cheese

Dutch Pancake with Spiced Fruit Mélange

Pear and Blue Cheese Pizzas

BLACK BEAN CHEESECAKE WITH SALSA

This savory cheesecake can also be served in smaller pieces as an appetizer or first course. It can also be served at room temperature, rather than heating as the recipe directs. Make it a day in advance, as overnight chilling is essential.

4 flour tortillas

3 packages (8 ounces each) reduced-fat cream cheese, room temperature

6 eggs, *or* 1 ½ cups no-cholesterol egg product

1 can (15 ounces) black beans, rinsed, drained

½ jalapeño chili, finely chopped

3 teaspoons minced garlic

2 teaspoons Worcestershire sauce

2 teaspoons dried cumin

½ teaspoon dried oregano leaves

½ teaspoon salt

½ teaspoon cayenne pepper

1 cup mild, *or* medium, salsa

PREPARATION TIME:
10–15 minutes
BAKING TIME:
1 ¾–2 hours
SERVINGS: *8*

Lightly grease 9-inch springform pan and line with overlapping tortillas.

Beat cream cheese in large bowl until smooth; beat in eggs. Mix in remaining ingredients, except salsa. Transfer mixture to prepared springform pan.

Bake at 300 degrees until center is set and sharp knife inserted halfway between center and edge of cheesecake comes out almost clean, 1 ¾ to 2 hours. Cool to room temperature on wire rack. Refrigerate overnight.

Cook wedges of cheesecake in lightly greased large skillet over medium-low heat until browned, 2 to 3 minutes on each side. Serve with salsa.

PER SERVING:
Calories: 276
Protein (g): 21.8
Carbohydrate (g): 23.3
Fat (g): 10.8
Saturated Fat (g): 5
Cholesterol (mg): 176.8
Dietary Fiber (g): 4.1
Sodium (mg): 1135

SWEET POTATO CHIPOTLE CHILI

V

PREPARATION TIME:
10–15 minutes
COOKING TIME:
15–20 minutes
SERVINGS: 4
(1½ cups each)

Chiptole chilies are dried, smoked jalapeño chilies. When canned, they are in adobo sauce, which is made with ground chilies and spices. They add a distinctive smoky flavor to this robust chili; taste before adding a second chili, as they can be fiercely hot in flavor!

2	cups frozen stir-fry pepper blend
1	teaspoon minced garlic
1–2	teaspoons minced gingerroot
1	teaspoon cumin seeds
1–2	tablespoons peanut, *or vegetable*, oil
3	cups cubed (½ inch), peeled sweet potatoes
1	can (14½ ounces) chili-style chunky tomatoes, undrained
2	cans (15 ounces each) black beans, rinsed, drained
1–2	chipotle chilies in adobo sauce, chopped
1	cup water, *or vegetable broth*
	Salt, to taste

Saute pepper blend, garlic, gingerroot, and cumin seeds in oil in large saucepan until tender, about 5 minutes.

Add remaining ingredients, except salt, to saucepan; heat to boiling. Reduce heat and simmer, covered, until potatoes are tender, about 15 minutes. Season to taste with salt.

PER SERVING:
Calories: 378
Protein (g): 16.2
Carbohydrate (g): 68.8
Fat (g): 5.4
Saturated Fat (g): 0.6
Cholesterol (mg): 0
Dietary Fiber (g): 16.9
Sodium (mg): 938

CURRIED COUCOUS WITH SMOKED TOFU

A delicious combination of flavors and textures. Serve with a green salad and crusty bread.

L

PREPARATION TIME:
10–15 minutes
COOKING TIME:
10–15 minutes
SERVINGS: *6*
(about 1 cup each)

½	cup finely chopped onion
½	cup finely chopped red, *or* green, bell pepper
1½	teaspoons minced garlic
1	tablespoon olive oil
1½	teaspoons curry powder
1¼	cups vegetable broth
1	package (10 ounces) couscous
2	packages (6 ounces each) smoked tofu, cubed
1	can (11 ounces) Mandarin orange segments, drained
	Salt and pepper, to taste
6	tablespoons (1½ ounces) crumbled reduced-fat feta cheese

Saute onion, bell pepper, and garlic in oil in medium saucepan until tender, about 5 minutes. Stir in curry powder; cook 1 to 2 minutes longer, stirring constantly.

Add broth to saucepan; heat to boiling. Stir in couscous (discard spice packet) and tofu; remove from heat and let stand, covered, 5 minutes. Stir in orange segments; season to taste with salt and pepper.

Spoon couscous mixture into serving bowl; sprinkle with cheese.

PER SERVING:
Calories: 293
Protein (g): 13.4
Carbohydrate (g): 45.1
Fat (g): 6.4
Saturated Fat (g): 1.3
Cholesterol (mg): 2.5
Dietary Fiber (g): 2.9
Sodium (mg): 352

POTATO GNOCCHI WITH SAGE CREAM

A rich, creamy sauce flavors the gnocchi in this dish.

PREPARATION TIME:

10 minutes

COOKING TIME:

18–22 minutes

SERVINGS: *6*

    2   cups whole milk
    1   teaspoon dried sage leaves
    1   cup chopped onion
  2–3   teaspoons margarine
    4   cups small broccoflower, *or* broccoli, florets
  1/2   cup water, divided
    1   package (16 ounces) potato gnocchi, cooked, warm
    2   tablespoons all-purpose flour
  1/2   teaspoon ground nutmeg
        Salt and pepper to taste
        Shredded Parmesan cheese, for garnish

PER SERVING:
Calories: 254
Protein (g): 10
Carbohydrate (g): 42.3
Fat (g): 5.4
Saturated Fat (g): 2.6
Cholesterol (mg): 16.6
Dietary Fiber (g): 4.1
Sodium (mg): 403

Heat milk and sage leaves to boiling in medium saucepan; reduce heat and simmer 10 minutes.

Saute onion in margarine in large skillet 2 to 3 minutes; add broccoflower and 1/4 cup water and heat to boiling. Reduce heat and simmer, covered, until broccoflower is tender and water gone, 5 to 8 minutes.

While vegetables are cooking, cook gnocchi according to package directions; add to vegetables in skillet.

Heat milk and sage mixture to boiling. Mix flour, nutmeg, and remaining 1/4 cup water; whisk into milk. Boil, whisking constantly, until thickened, about 1 minute. Pour sauce over vegetables and gnocchi in skillet and season to taste with salt and pepper. Spoon into serving bowl; sprinkle with Parmesan cheese.

CHEESE AND VEGETABLE RISOTTO PANCAKES

A perfect recipe for using leftover risotto. Top each serving with a poached or fried egg for a hearty brunch or light supper.

Vegetable cooking spray
1/2 cup chopped onion
1 cup arborio rice
2 1/2 cups vegetable broth
1/2 cup dry white wine
1 cup (4 ounces) shredded Parmesan cheese
1/4–1/2 cup (1–2 ounces) crumbled blue cheese
4 egg whites, *or* 1/2 cup no-cholesterol egg product
6 canned artichoke hearts, coarsely chopped
1/4 cup coarsely chopped roasted red pepper
Salt and pepper, to taste
Finely chopped parsley, for garnish

PREPARATION TIME:

5 minutes

COOKING TIME:

35–40 minutes

SERVINGS: 4

Spray large saucepan with cooking spray; heat over medium heat until hot. Add onion and saute 2 minutes. Add rice to saucepan; cook over medium heat until beginning to brown, 3 to 4 minutes.

Add vegetable broth and wine to saucepan; heat to boiling. Reduce heat and simmer, covered, until rice is tender and liquid absorbed, about 20 to 25 minutes, stirring occasionally. Remove from heat; stir in cheeses, egg whites, artichoke hearts, and red pepper. Season to taste with salt and pepper.

Spray two 10-inch skillets generously with cooking spray; heat over medium heat until hot. Spoon half the risotto mixture into each skillet, shaping into large pancakes. Cook over medium heat until lightly browned on the bottoms, 5 to 8 minutes. Invert pancakes onto plates; slide back into skillets and cook until lightly browned on other side, 5 to 8 minutes. Cut pancakes in half; invert onto serving plates and sprinkle with parsley.

PER SERVING:
Calories: 382
Protein (g): 18.8
Carbohydrate (g): 52.1
Fat (g): 8.4
Saturated Fat (g): 5.2
Cholesterol (mg): 21.1
Dietary Fiber (g): 3.9
Sodium (mg): 625

FETTUCCINE FLORENTINE TIMBALE

PREP/COOK TIME:
20–25 minutes
BAKING TIME:
55–60 minutes
SERVINGS: **6**

PER SERVING:
Calories: 337
Protein (g): 22.8
Carbohydrate (g): 46.9
Fat (g): 5.8
Saturated Fat (g): 2.2
Cholesterol (mg): 20
Dietary Fiber (g): 1.6
Sodium (mg): 587

An impressive looking entrée for entertaining or special family meals. Assemble the dish in advance, then relax with guests while dinner is baking.

12	ounces florentine, *or* spinach, fettuccine
	Vegetable cooking spray
6	tablespoons dry unseasoned bread crumbs, divided
1	package (1.8 ounces) white sauce mix
2 1/4	cups non-fat milk
1 1/4	cups (5 ounces) shredded reduced-fat Italian 6-cheese blend, divided
1	package (10 ounces) frozen chopped spinach, thawed, well drained
1	cup fat-free cottage cheese
	Salt and pepper, to taste
1/2	cup roasted red peppers, drained

Cook fettuccine according to package directions.

Spray 9-inch springform pan with cooking spray; coat with 3 tablespoons bread crumbs. Make white sauce mix according to package directions, using milk; stir in 1/2 cup shredded cheese. Stir sauce into pasta. Spoon 1/2 the pasta mixture into prepared pan.

Mix spinach, 1/2 cup shredded cheese, and cottage cheese; season to taste with salt and pepper. Spoon spinach mixture evenly over pasta in pan. Arrange red peppers over spinach mixture; top with remaining pasta mixture. Combine remaining 3 tablespoons bread crumbs and remaining 1/4 cup shredded cheese; sprinkle over pasta.

Bake, uncovered, at 375 degrees until golden, 55 to 60 minutes. Let stand 10 minutes; loosen side of pan with sharp knife and remove. Cut into wedges.

TIP:

To quickly thaw the spinach, pierce package in 2 or 3 places with sharp knife and place on microwave-safe plate; microwave at high power 3 to 4 minutes.

ARTICHOKE TORTELLINI BAKE

Refrigerated fresh tortellini and ravioli are convenient to have on hand for speedy meal preparation—use any favorite kind in this dish.

L

PREP/COOK TIME:
15–20 minutes
BAKING TIME:
20 minutes
SERVINGS: 4

  1 package (9 ounces) mozzarella-garlic tortellini
     Vegetable cooking spray
  2 cups (4 ounces) sliced mushrooms
  1 small onion, sliced
  1 teaspoon minced garlic
  2 tablespoons flour
  1 cup non-fat milk
     Salt and cayenne pepper, to taste
  1 can (14 ounces) artichoke hearts, drained
½–1 cup (2–4 ounces) shredded reduced-fat Italian 6-cheese blend, divided
1–2 tablespoons seasoned dry bread crumbs

Cook tortellini according to package directions.

Spray large saucepan with cooking spray; heat over medium heat until hot. Saute mushrooms, onion, and garlic until tender, about 5 minutes. Stir in flour; cook 1 to 2 minutes. Add milk and heat to boiling; boil, stirring constantly, until thickened, 1 to 2 minutes. Season to taste with salt and cayenne pepper.

Stir in artichokes, tortellini, and all but 2 tablespoons of the cheese. Pour into greased 1½-quart casserole; sprinkle with bread crumbs and remaining 2 tablespoons cheese.

Bake at 350 degrees until bubbly and browned on the top, about 20 minutes.

PER SERVING:
Calories: 267
Protein (g): 16.9
Carbohydrate (g): 37.4
Fat (g): 6.4
Saturated Fat (g): 3.4
Cholesterol (mg): 28.6
Dietary Fiber (g): 1.5
Sodium (mg): 523

VIETNAMESE CURRIED VEGETABLE AND COCONUT STEW

PREP/COOK TIME:

25–30 minutes

SERVINGS: *6 (about 1 1/2 cups each)*

Rice stick noodles, made with rice flour, can be round or flat. They must be softened in water before cooking. Angel hair pasta can be substituted.

Vegetable cooking spray
2 cups frozen stir-fry pepper blend
2 tablespoons minced gingerroot
1 tablespoon minced garlic
3–4 tablespoons curry powder
3 1/2 cups vegetable broth
3 cups reduced-fat coconut milk
1 tablespoon grated lime rind
1 teaspoon oriental chili paste
1 cup broccoli florets
1 cup cubed, peeled, seeded acorn, *or* butternut, squash
1/2 package (8-ounce size) rice stick noodles
1/4 cup all-purpose flour
1/4 cup cold water
1/4 cup lime juice
Salt, to taste
Finely chopped cilantro, for garnish

Spray large saucepan with cooking spray; heat over medium heat until hot. Saute pepper blend, gingerroot, and garlic 5 minutes. Stir in curry powder and cook 1 minute longer.

Add broth, coconut milk, lime rind, and chili paste to saucepan; heat to boiling. Add vegetables; reduce heat and simmer, covered, until vegetables are tender, about 15 minutes.

While stew is cooking, place noodles in large bowl; pour cold water over to cover. Let stand until noodles are separate and soft, about 5 minutes. Stir noodles into 4 quarts boiling water in large saucepan. Reduce heat and simmer, uncovered, until tender, about 5 minutes; drain.

Heat stew to boiling. Mix flour, water, and lime juice; stir into boiling stew. Boil, stirring constantly, until thickened, about 1 minute. Season to taste with salt.

Serve stew over noodles in shallow bowls; sprinkle generously with cilantro.

PER SERVING:
Calories: 204
Protein (g): 5.2
Carbohydrate (g): 32.8
Fat (g): 7.2
Saturated Fat (g): 0.1
Cholesterol (mg): 0
Dietary Fiber (g): 4
Sodium (mg): 627

ROASTED VEGETABLES, MOO SHU STYLE

PREPARATION TIME:
15–20 minutes
BAKING TIME:
25 minutes
SERVINGS: *6 (2 each)*

PER SERVING:
Calories: 426
Protein (g): 16.6
Carbohydrate (g): 79.1
Fat (g): 6
Saturated Fat (g): 0.9
Cholesterol (mg): 0
Dietary Fiber (g): 8.8
Sodium (mg): 363

For simplicity, we've substituted flour tortillas for the Mandarin pancakes traditionally served with Moo Shu dishes.

   Vegetable cooking spray
  1 pound Chinese long beans, *or* snow peas
  1 pound mushrooms, sliced
  4 medium zucchini, cut lengthwise into halves, sliced
  1 medium onion, thinly sliced
¾–1 teaspoon 5-spice powder
   Salt and pepper, to taste
 12 flour tortillas
  ¾ cup plum sauce
  2 cups fresh, *or* canned, drained, bean sprouts
  2 medium carrots, shredded
   Fresh cilantro leaves, for garnish

Spray aluminum foil-lined jelly roll pan with cooking spray. Cut long beans into 2-inch pieces. Arrange beans, mushrooms, zucchini, and onion in single layer on pan. Spray vegetables generously with cooking spray and sprinkle with 5-spice powder.

Roast vegetables at 425 degrees until crisp-tender, about 25 minutes. Combine vegetables in bowl; season to taste with salt and pepper.

To serve, spread 1 tablespoon plum sauce in center of each tortilla. Spoon roasted vegetables onto tortillas; top with bean sprouts, carrots, and cilantro leaves and roll up, tucking up one end to hold.

SZECHUAN VEGETABLE STIR-FRY

The hot chili oil is HOT, so begin with less, adding more to your taste. Sesame oil can be substituted for the hot chili oil. Serve this stir-fry with rice or Chinese noodles.

PREP/COOK TIME:
35–40 minutes
SERVINGS: *4*
(about 1¼ cups each)

1 cup vegetable broth, divided
⅓ cup orange juice
¼ cup tamari soy sauce
1–2 teaspoons hot chili oil
1 package (8 ounces) tempeh, *or* light firm tofu, cut into ¾-inch cubes
1 tablespoon sesame, *or* peanut, oil
8 ounces asparagus, cut into 1½-inch pieces
1 cup sliced carrots
1½ cups frozen stir-fry pepper blend
2–3 teaspoons minced gingerroot
2 teaspoons minced garlic
½ cup sliced shiitake, *or* cremini, mushrooms
2 tablespoons cornstarch
Salt, to taste
¼ cup peanuts, optional

Combine ½ cup broth, orange juice, soy sauce, and hot chili oil; pour over tempeh in shallow glass dish and let stand 20 minutes. Drain, reserving marinade. Prepare other ingredients while tempeh is standing.

Stir-fry tempeh in sesame oil in wok or large skillet 2 to 3 minutes. Add asparagus, carrots, pepper blend, gingerroot, and garlic; stir-fry until vegetables are crisp-tender, 8 to 10 minutes. Add mushrooms; stir-fry 3 to 4 minutes longer.

Add reserved marinade to wok; heat to boiling. Mix cornstarch and remaining ½ cup broth; stir into boiling mixture. Boil, stirring constantly, until thickened, about 1 minute. Season to taste with salt.

Spoon mixture into serving bowl; sprinkle with peanuts, if using.

PER SERVING:
Calories: 239
Protein (g): 16.9
Carbohydrate (g): 25.2
Fat (g): 9.6
Saturated Fat (g): 1.4
Cholesterol (mg): 0
Dietary Fiber (g): 7.5
Sodium (mg): 1277

TEMPEH STEAK WITH RED AND GREEN STIR-FRY

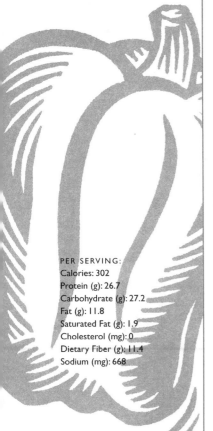

PREP/COOK TIME:

20–25 minutes

SERVINGS: *6*

(about 1 cup each)

If available, use red or rhubarb Swiss chard for its beautiful red and green color.

 2 cups sliced red onions
 1 cup sliced celery
 2 teaspoons minced garlic
 1 teaspoon minced gingerroot
 1 tablespoon peanut oil
 6 cups thinly sliced Swiss chard, *or* spinach
 2 cups sliced red, *or* green, bell peppers
 2 cups vegetable broth
 2 tablespoons cornstarch
 4 teaspoons tamari soy sauce, divided
½–¾ teaspoon hot chili paste
 3 packages (8 ounces each) tempeh, cut into halves

Stir-fry onions, celery, garlic, and gingerroot in oil in wok or large skillet 1 to 2 minutes. Add Swiss chard and stir-fry 1 to 2 minutes. Add bell peppers to wok; stir-fry until vegetables are crisp-tender, 2 to 3 minutes.

Combine broth, cornstarch, 2 teaspoons tamari, and chili paste; stir into wok. Heat to boiling; boil, stirring constantly, until thickened, about 1 minute.

Brush tempeh with remaining 2 teaspoons tamari. Cook tempeh in greased large skillet over medium heat until browned, 2 to 3 minutes on each side.

Arrange tempeh on serving platter; spoon vegetable mixture over.

PER SERVING:
Calories: 302
Protein (g): 26.7
Carbohydrate (g): 27.2
Fat (g): 11.8
Saturated Fat (g): 1.9
Cholesterol (mg): 0
Dietary Fiber (g): 11.4
Sodium (mg): 668

GINGER COCONUT RICE AND SWEET POTATOES

Jasmine rice scented with lemon grass and coconut is an Asian-inspired entrée offering.

Vegetable cooking spray
1/2 cup finely chopped onion
1 1/2–2 tablespoons minced gingerroot
1–1 1/2 tablespoons minced lemon grass
1 teaspoon minced garlic
1 1/4 cups water
1 1/4 cups reduced-fat coconut milk
1 cup jasmine, *or* long-grain, rice
1 sweet potato, peeled, quartered, cut into 1/4-inch slices
2 cups frozen vegetable stir-fry blend with asparagus
1/4 cup loosely packed cilantro, finely chopped
1–2 tablespoons lime juice
Salt and pepper, to taste

Spray large saucepan with cooking spray; heat over medium heat until hot. Saute onion, gingerroot, lemon grass, and garlic until onion is tender, about 5 minutes. Stir in water, coconut milk, rice, and sweet potato; heat to boiling. Reduce heat and simmer, covered, 10 minutes.

Mix in stir-fry blend; cook, covered, until vegetables are tender and liquid absorbed, 8 to 10 minutes. Stir in cilantro; season to taste with lime juice and salt and pepper.

V

PREPARATION TIME:
10–15 minutes
COOKING TIME:
20–25 minutes
SERVINGS: *4*
(about 1 cup each)

PER SERVING:
Calories: 274
Protein (g): 5
Carbohydrate (g): 53.6
Fat (g): 3.9
Saturated Fat (g): 0
Cholesterol (mg): 0
Dietary Fiber (g): 3.7
Sodium (mg): 18

VEGETABLE STRUDEL WITH CHEESE

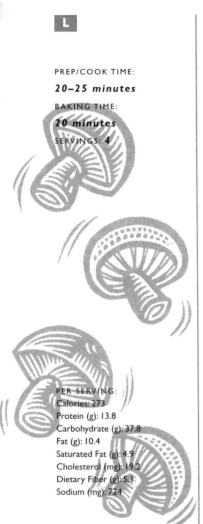

PREP/COOK TIME:
20–25 minutes
BAKING TIME:
20 minutes
SERVINGS: 4

A special dish for festive occasions that's easy enough for family dinners, too.

1½ cups cubed, peeled, seeded butternut, *or* acorn, squash
1½ cups small broccoli florets
 2 packages (1¼ ounces each) cheese sauce mix, divided
 1 cup sliced shiitake, *or* cremini, mushrooms
 ½ cup chopped red, *or* green, bell pepper
 ½ cup chopped yellow, *or* green, bell pepper
 ¼ cup chopped shallot
 1 teaspoon minced garlic
 2 teaspoons margarine
 ¾ cup (3 ounces) shredded reduced-fat brick, *or* Swiss, cheese
   Salt and pepper, to taste
 5 sheets frozen, thawed fillo pastry
   Vegetable cooking spray

PER SERVING:
Calories: 273
Protein (g): 13.8
Carbohydrate (g): 37.8
Fat (g): 10.4
Saturated Fat (g): 4.9
Cholesterol (mg): 19.2
Dietary Fiber (g): 5.1
Sodium (mg): 724

Cook squash and broccoli, covered, in 1 inch simmering water until tender, about 10 minutes; drain. Make cheese sauce according to package directions.

Saute mushrooms, bell peppers, shallot, and garlic in margarine in large skillet 5 minutes. Stir in squash, broccoli, and half the cheese sauce. Remove from heat and stir in cheese; season to taste with salt and pepper.

Lay 1 sheet fillo on clean towel on table; spray generously with cooking spray. Cover with second sheet fillo and spray generously with cooking spray; repeat with remaining fillo.

Spoon vegetable mixture along long edge of fillo, 3 to 4 inches from the edge. Fold **edge** of fillo over filling and roll up, using towel to help lift and roll; place seam side down on greased cookie sheet. Spray top of fillo generously with cooking spray.

Bake at 400 degrees until golden, about 20 minutes. Let stand 5 minutes before cutting. Trim ends; cut strudel into 4 pieces and arrange on plates. Serve with remaining cheese sauce.

DUTCH PANCAKE WITH SPICED FRUIT MÉLANGE

A spectacular brunch or lunch entrée that will win raves!

Dutch Pancake (recipe follows)
Butter-flavored vegetable cooking spray
3 medium tart cooking apples, unpeeled, cored, sliced
1 cup mixed dried fruit
¼ cup dried cranberries, *or* cherries
¼ cup sugar
½ cup orange juice
1 teaspoon ground cinnamon
Maple syrup, warm, optional

LO

PREP/COOK TIME:
20–25 minutes
BAKING TIME:
20–25 minutes
SERVINGS: *4*

Make Dutch Pancake.

Spray large skillet with cooking spray; heat over medium heat until hot. Add apples to skillet and cook 2 to 3 minutes. Add remaining ingredients, except maple syrup, and cook, covered, over medium heat until apples are just tender, 8 to 10 minutes. Heat to boiling and cook, uncovered, until liquid is syrupy, 2 to 3 minutes.

Spoon fruit mixture into warm Dutch Pancake; cut into wedges and serve with maple syrup, if desired.

DUTCH PANCAKE

2 eggs
½ cup no-cholesterol egg product, *or* 4 egg whites
¾ cup non-fat milk
¾ cup all-purpose flour
1 tablespoon sugar
¼ teaspoon salt
2 tablespoons margarine

149

Whisk all ingredients, except margarine, in large bowl until almost smooth (batter will be slightly lumpy).

Heat margarine in large skillet with ovenproof handle until melted and bubbly; pour in batter. Bake, uncovered, at 425 degrees until pancake is puffed and browned, 20 to 25 minutes (do not open door during first 15 minutes). Serve warm.

PER SERVING:
Calories: 465
Protein (g): 11.7
Carbohydrate (g): 88.4
Fat (g): 9.1
Saturated Fat (g): 2.1
Cholesterol (mg): 106.8
Dietary Fiber (g): 6.4
Sodium (mg): 321

PEAR AND BLUE CHEESE PIZZAS

A unique brunch offering; serve with mesclun salad and a light raspberry dressing.

L

    1 package (1 pound, 13 ounces) large reduced-fat buttermilk biscuits
    1 cup cubed (½ inch) unpeeled, cored ripe pears
    ¼ cup raisins
  2–3 tablespoons chopped walnuts
    2 tablespoons sugar
  ½–1 cup (2–4 ounces) crumbled blue cheese

Roll biscuits into 6-inch rounds and place on greased baking sheet. Combine pears, raisins, walnuts, and sugar in bowl; spoon onto biscuits and sprinkle with blue cheese.

Bake at 350 degrees until biscuits are browned, 18 to 20 minutes.

PREPARATION TIME:
10–15 minutes
BAKING TIME:
18–20 minutes
SERVINGS: *8*

PER SERVING:
Calories: 400
Protein (g): 9
Carbohydrate (g): 57.1
Fat (g): 15.1
Saturated Fat (g): 4.8
Cholesterol (mg): 5.3
Dietary Fiber (g): 2.5
Sodium (mg): 1144

index